GRAND PRIX CIRCUITS

GRAND
ALAN HENRY

PRIX CIRCUITS

A TOUR OF FORMULA 1 CIRCUITS FROM STARTING GRID TO CHEQUERED FLAG

Weidenfeld & Nicolson
London

CONTENTS

INTRODUCTION

T HE GRAND PRIX CIRCUITS OF THE WORLD HAVE COME TO BE REGARDED AS
SHRINES TO THIS MOST COLOURFUL OF 20TH-CENTURY SPORTS – HALLOWED
RIBBONS OF TARMAC ON WHICH THE HIGH-OCTANE CONTEST FOR THE
FORMULA 1 WORLD CHAMPIONSHIP IS FOUGHT OUT WITH CALCULATED
PRECISION EACH AND EVERY YEAR.

They are as Wimbledon to the lawn-tennis fraternity, Cardiff Arms Park to the rugby world or The Oval to test cricketers. Each circuit throws up its own very specialized and individual challenge to that handful of select competitors who have graduated to the sport's most senior and spectacular category.

The tracks in this book are those on which it is planned to run the 1997 FIA Formula 1 World Championship. These range from long-established Monza and Silverstone to the new Austrian A1-Ring. At the time of going to press, not all races had been run, and some track records may have been bettered.

Ask half a dozen Grand Prix drivers for their favourite circuit and, like as not, you will receive the same number of replies. Some love the precision required at Monaco, others the high-speed self-discipline imposed by Spa-Francorchamps, the passionately enthusiastic atmosphere at Monza, the variety of corners at Melbourne or the swooping curves of Suzuka. Whatever the answer, all competing teams know only too well that the circuits included on the Championship trail require exacting standards of versatility and consistency from the men who are strapped into the cockpits.

Unlike the venues for other international sports, Grand Prix circuits are always changing. The centre court at Wimbledon and the grandstands at Wembley may benefit from a lick or paint or a new public-address system, but otherwise they remain substantially unchanged year in, year out. A Grand Prix circuit, however, must evolve and adapt to changing circumstances.

As the speed of Formula 1 cars increases, so the sport's governing body may seek to rein in their performance by means of changes in the technical regulations. Yet much of the burden of trying to minimize the risks of an inherently hazardous sport inevitably falls on the individual circuit owners.

Run-off areas have to be increased to halt wayward competitors with the minimum prospect of damage to the drivers. Corners have to be reprofiled, chicanes installed and track surfaces improved. Paddock facilities must now be impeccable, and the image of high-technology machines being readied for battle in gravel-strewn compounds has become a distant memory. Now there are permanent garage complexes facing out on to the pit lane with heating, light and security for the mechanics and engineers.

Formula 1 motor racing now ranks in the top handful of televised global sports and its crisp, well-scrubbed image calls not only for circuits equipped to the highest possible standards, but the sport must also be presented in a way calculated to enhance its five-star image among corporate investors.

The portraits of the various international circuits contained in this book are intended to offer readers a feel for the individual atmosphere of each, a taste of their history and the prospects for the best possible racing in the future. As an obvious sub-text, the profiles also serve to chart the dramatic progress in motor-racing safety made over the past generation, while, at the same time, serving as a stark reminder that this is a pastime that will always involve flirting with danger.

The wide open sweeps of the epic Österreichring circuit, which was last used to host the Austrian Grand Prix in 1987. In 1997 a totally revamped track, shortened and updated in order to meet current safety standards, replaced it.

ALBERT PARK, MELBOURNE

CIRCUIT LENGTH:
3.294 miles (5.301km).
LAP RECORD:
Heinz-Harald Frentzen
(3.0 Williams-Renault FW19), 1m 30.585s,
139.929mph (225.187kmph).
Lap record established in 1997.

CIRCUIT ASSESSMENT by MARTIN BRUNDLE:

'A great circuit, but I'm just sorry that I didn't last longer in the race, having a shunt on the first lap and then spinning off on the first lap of the restart when I took the spare car. Lots of interesting corners, but difficult to sustain sufficient grip and work out the optimum chassis balance here.'

MELBOURNE'S ALBERT PARK CIRCUIT ORIGINALLY ATTRACTED INTERNATIONAL RECOGNITION IN 1956, THE YEAR IN WHICH THE CITY HOSTED THE OLYMPIC GAMES, WHEN A GOOD FIELD OF CONTEMPORARY F1 CARS WAS ATTRACTED TO AUSTRALIA. STIRLING MOSS DRIVING A MASERATI EMERGED AS THE WINNER OF A NON-CHAMPIONSHIP RACE TO CELEBRATE THIS GREAT SPORTING OCCASION.

After this event, the race track fell into disuse and disrepair. However, when the state of Victoria won the battle to stage the now World-Championship-status Australian Grand Prix from 1996 onwards – thereby depriving South Australia of its splendidly popular Adelaide fixture – the Albert Park circuit was completely revamped and brought up to the level required for a front-line international forum.

Although the motor-racing fraternity was highly impressed with the effort put into reviving Albert Park, the arrival of top-class Formula 1 racing in Melbourne did not attract the unqualified approval of all the local citizenry.

A vocal minority of so-called conservationists took exception to what they regarded as the ecological

The Williams FW18s of Jacques Villeneuve and Damon Hill lead the pack off on the final pre-race parade lap prior to the 1996 Australian GP at Melbourne.

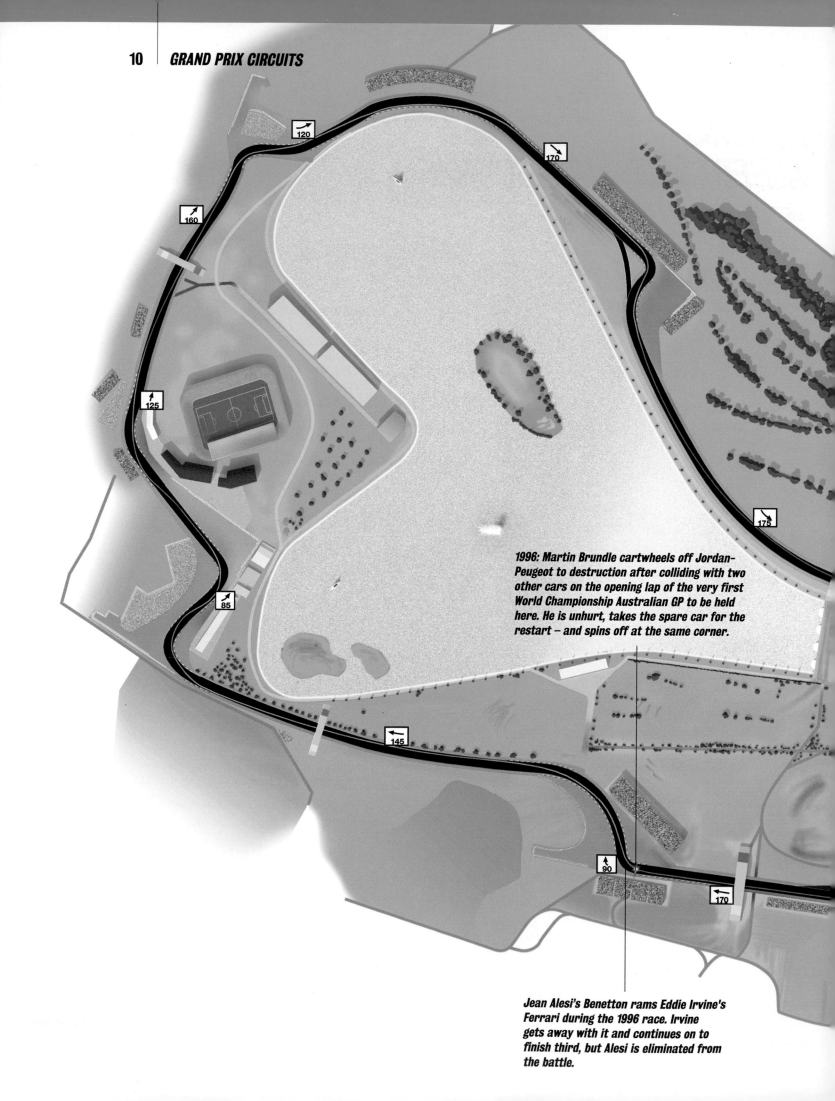

120

170

160

125

175

85

1996: Martin Brundle cartwheels off Jordan-
Peugeot to destruction after colliding with two
other cars on the opening lap of the very first
World Championship Australian GP to be held
here. He is unhurt, takes the spare car for the
restart – and spins off at the same corner.

145

90

170

Jean Alesi's Benetton rams Eddie Irvine's
Ferrari during the 1996 race. Irvine
gets away with it and continues on to
finish third, but Alesi is eliminated from
the battle.

AUSTRALIAN GRAND PRIX
ALBERT PARK, MELBOURNE

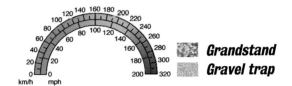

Grandstand
Gravel trap

CIRCUIT LENGTH:
3.294 miles (5.301km)

 = mph

Michael Schumacher's Ferrari
passed Irvine's sister car to take
third place behind the Williams-Renaults
in the opening stages of the 1996 race.
But it proved a vain chase, since
Schumacher retired later with a gearbox
oil leak.

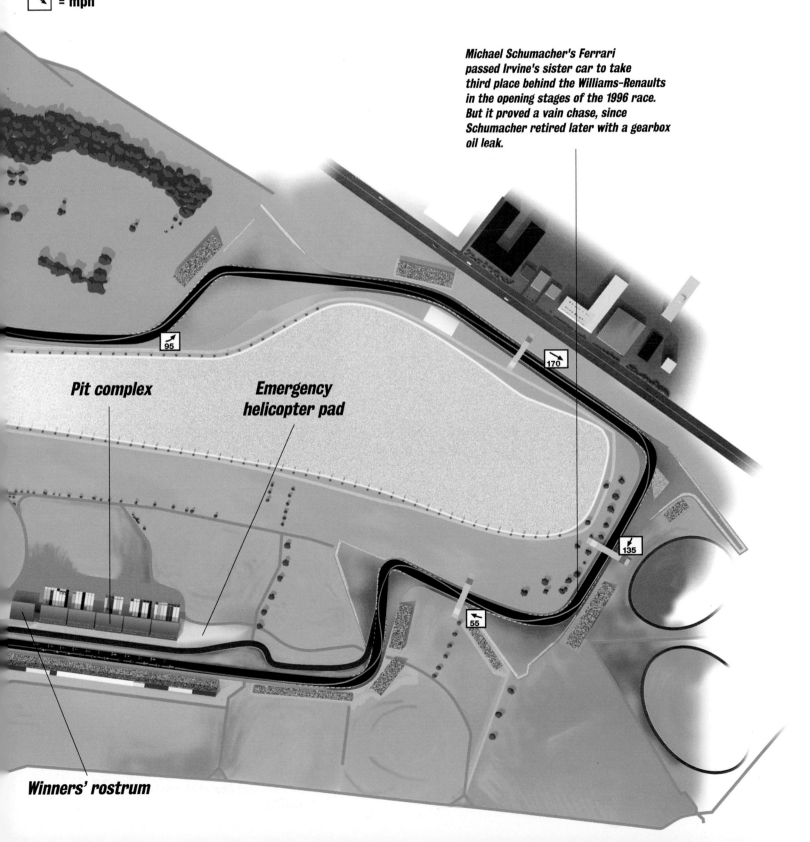

Pit complex

**Emergency
helicopter pad**

95

170

135

55

Winners' rostrum

vandalism of, in their opinion, an attractive public park. It has to be recorded that this viewpoint hardly accorded with the majority of local opinion, which was that the venue had been allowed to degenerate into something of a wasteland in recent years and that the investment in the new circuit had, in fact, spruced the place up considerably.

'Taxpayers slugged $80 million just for a motor race' ran one advertisement in a local newspaper. 'Join the March! Sunday 10 March, 1pm.' According to the protesters, the Victoria state government had wasted $55 million of public money 'chainsawing down more than 1,000 trees, pouring 42,000 square metres of bitumen, erecting ugly pit buildings and gouging underpasses'.

Yet the race went ahead without being disrupted by any protesters and it certainly was a terrific event. Indycar champion Jacques Villeneuve opened the 1996 World Championship season by shaking the Formula 1 community to its foundations, not only qualifying his Williams FW18 on pole position, but also coming within a few miles of winning on his maiden Grand Prix outing.

Granted, he was probably the best prepared novice in the sport's history – with more than 5,500 miles (9,000km) of testing under his belt since it was originally announced he would quit Indycar for F1 the previous August – but none of that could detract from the reality that the French-Canadian youngster certainly marked himself out as the sport's most impressive newcomer since Michael Schumacher's arrival on the scene less than five years earlier.

Yet the race victory eventually fell to Villeneuve's team-mate Damon Hill in the other Williams. As

David Coulthard's McLaren-Mercedes practising for the '96 Australian GP against the backdrop of the picturesque lake round which the Albert Park circuit is laid out.

Villeneuve slowed with fading oil pressure, it was left to the vastly more experienced Englishman to pick up where he had left off in Adelaide the previous November, and start the new season with a win. Hill had driven with great restraint and sympathy for his car, balancing aggression with the obvious need to avoid a collision with his dazzling new team-mate, whom he had been shadowing from the start.

'I would say this was a very mature performance from both drivers,' said Williams's technical director Patrick Head, obviously very satisfied to have started the season with another 1-2.

Villeneuve took the lead from the start, and even though the race was red-flagged at the end of the opening lap, following a shunt involving Martin Brundle's Jordan, he repeated his brilliant getaway from the front of the grid when the race was restarted.

For 53 of the 58 laps, Villeneuve led. He lost the advantage only briefly to his team-mate Hill when the two Williams-Renaults came in for their routine, single refuelling stops. Yet for many laps Jacques's Williams had been trailing an ominous haze of oil smoke, leaving streaks of lubricant all over Hill's sister car in its wake.

With just six laps left to run, Patrick Head, the Williams team's technical director was shouting over the radio link to warn Villeneuve that his oil pressure was fading. Two laps later, Jacques saw the red oil warning light begin to flicker ominously in the corners. He had no choice, either ease back or watch, with almost certainty, as his engine blew up.

At the end of the day, the drivers were practically unreserved in their praise for the Albert Park circuit. It combined a wide variety of corners with several overtaking opportunities on each lap, including the end of the start/finish straight and the entry to a fast right-hander midway around the lap where Martin Brundle had cartwheeled over the top of several other cars on the opening lap of this particular event.

A year later Brundle was back in Melbourne in a new role as Murray Walker's partner in the commentary box for ITV, his F1 career having come to an end. He now had the task of commenting on the circumstances that led to David Coulthard opening the 1997 World Championship with a convincing victory for the McLaren-Mercedes team. The Scot remained cool under pressure from both Schumacher's Ferrari and Heinz-Harald Frentzen's Williams in the closing stages to win by 20 seconds from Schumacher after Frentzen spun out of second place after a brake drum exploded with just a couple of laps left to run.

Mika Hakkinen's McLaren-Mercedes speeds through the leafy environs of Melbourne's Albert Park on its way to fifth place in the 1996 Australian Grand Prix.

BRAZIL

AUTODROMO JOSE CARLOS PACE, INTER- LAGOS, SÃO PAULO

CIRCUIT LENGTH:
2.667 miles (4.292km).
LAP RECORD:
Jacques Villeneuve
(3.0 Williams–Renault FW19), 1m 18.397s,
122.465mph (197.089kmph).
Lap record established in 1997.

CIRCUIT ASSESSMENT by JEAN ALESI:

'A very challenging circuit with a lot of quick corners in which the G-forces build up. Hard on the car, though, and quite difficult to work out a decent chassis balance. Exhilarating when everything goes well.'

ALTHOUGH BRAZIL DID NOT JOIN THE OFFICIAL F1 WORLD CHAMPIONSHIP TRAIL UNTIL 1973, THE INTERLAGOS CIRCUIT ON THE OUTSKIRTS OF SPRAWLING, METROPOLITAN SÃO PAULO HOSTED ITS FIRST RACE MEETING AS LONG AGO AS 1940. IN THE POST-WAR YEARS IT WAS A REGULAR VENUE FOR INTERNATIONAL SPORTS-CAR EVENTS, FREQUENTLY ATTRACTING COMPETITORS FROM EUROPE. BUT IT IS AS THE BREEDING GROUND FOR SUCH LEGENDARY BRAZILIAN DRIVERS AS EMERSON FITTIPALDI, NELSON PIQUET AND THE LATE AYRTON SENNA THAT REALLY GAINED THE CIRCUIT ITS INTERNATIONAL REPUTATION.

In contrast to Rio de Janeiro's cosmopolitan and sun-soaked image, São Paulo – Brazil's second city – is an unremarkable, semi-industrial conurbation. As its name suggests, Interlagos was built on an unde-veloped area surrounding a number of lakes on the edge of the city. Although it projects a somewhat ramshackle image, the original 4.95-mile (7.97-km) circuit configuration ensured that it came to be regarded as one of the most challenging in the world.

By the early 1970s, the progress of Emerson Fittipaldi, his elder brother Wilson, and Carlos Pace on the British F3 scene really started Brazil's F1

Michael Schumacher aims his Ferrari through one of the high-speed corners at São Paulo's Interlagos circuit. The German driver finished third in the 1996 Brazilian Grand Prix at this venue.

Ferra Dura

Plenty of action at the first corner in 1993. Michael Andretti's McLaren and Gerhard Berger's Ferrari got involved in a massive collision here only seconds after the start of the race, while, later in the event, Alain Prost's Williams skidded off the track during a cloudburst.

Pit complex

Descida Do Sol

Curva Do Sol

Emergency helicopter pad

CIRCUIT LENGTH:
2.667 miles (4.292km)

= mph

BRAZILIAN GRAND PRIX
AUTODROMO JOSE CARLOS PACE
INTERLAGOS, SÃO PAULO

Grandstand
Gravel trap

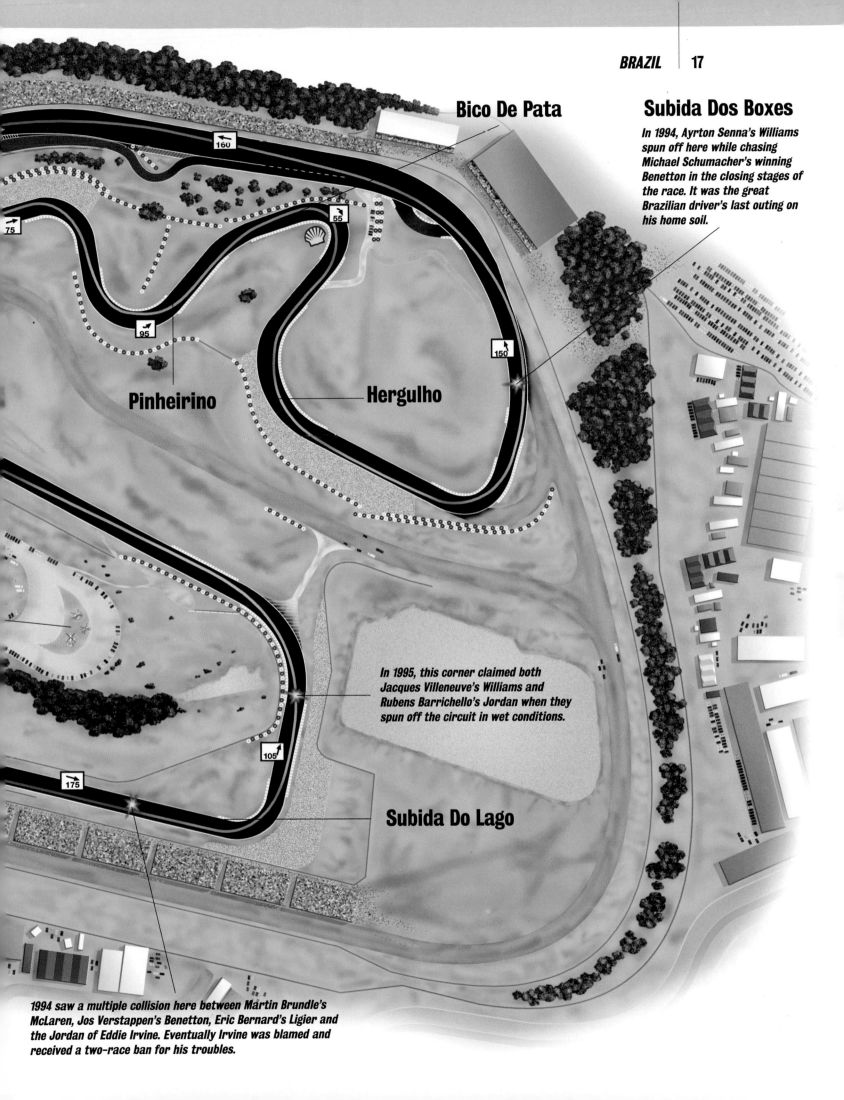

Bico De Pata

Subida Dos Boxes

In 1994, Ayrton Senna's Williams spun off here while chasing Michael Schumacher's winning Benetton in the closing stages of the race. It was the great Brazilian driver's last outing on his home soil.

Pinheirino

Hergulho

In 1995, this corner claimed both Jacques Villeneuve's Williams and Rubens Barrichello's Jordan when they spun off the circuit in wet conditions.

Subida Do Lago

1994 saw a multiple collision here between Martin Brundle's McLaren, Jos Verstappen's Benetton, Eric Bernard's Ligier and the Jordan of Eddie Irvine. Eventually Irvine was blamed and received a two-race ban for his troubles.

Interlagos – as its name suggests – is laid out around a complex of lakes on the fringes of São Paulo. Here, a Forti, Footwork and McLaren are seen in line astern during practice for the 1995 Brazilian GP.

bandwagon seriously rolling. In 1970, Interlagos was one of the circuits that hosted a round of the winter international F3 series, followed by F2 races in both 1971 and 1972. Easter 1972 also saw the first non-Championship F1 race held at Interlagos, won by Argentina's Carlos Reutemann in a Brabham BT34, but in the following year Emerson Fittipaldi delighted the hordes of passionately enthusiastic fans with a stupendous victory in the first World Championship Brazilian Grand Prix at the wheel of a Lotus.

Fittipaldi by then had become the sport's youngest ever World Champion at the age of 26. He would return to São Paulo at the end of the season to be fêted by millions in a civic parade through the city, and he was carrying the reigning title holder's coveted

score his second Brazilian GP success. But in 1975 he would be beaten into second place by his fellow *Paulista,* Carlos Pace, at the wheel of one of Bernie Ecclestone's works Brabham BT44s. Two years later, Pace would be killed in a light aircraft accident in Brazil and, much later, the Interlagos circuit would be renamed in his honour.

The great attraction for the spectators was the topography of the challenging São Paulo circuit. From the huge grandstands on the main start/finish straight, the view commanded virtually the entire track, with its daunting sequence of rising and plunging high-speed corners. During the 1970s, the Brazilian GP usually took place at the end of January, when conditions were at their very hottest, and it

'EXHILARATING WHEN EVERYTHING GOES WELL'

ed number one when he scored that memorable victory. The following year, having switched to the McLaren team, Fittipaldi was back at Interlagos to

became a tradition that the circuit fire crews would use their hoses to douse the fans in the bleachers in the excited run-up to the start of the race.

By this stage, however, Interlagos had changed considerably. New safety considerations meant that the track had been revamped and its lap distance considerably shortened to 2.687 miles (4.325km). As well, many of the superb high-speed corners had been consigned to history and the whole place somehow lacked the epic sense of occasion that had been an integral part of the Brazilian Grand Prix throughout the 1970s.

Overtaking also became rather more difficult on the new track, and the bottom of the hill beyond the pits is now the most obvious place at which to attempt a passing manoeuvre. However, this is an extremely quick section of the circuit and certainly not for the faint-hearted.

Yet the passionate fervour of the crowds remained undimmed and the fans turned out in force to celebrate two brilliant victories for Senna in 1991 and 1993, both of which were achieved at the wheel of a McLaren. In 1994, Senna switched to Williams and spun off on the tricky uphill right-hander before the pits while chasing Michael Schumacher's winning Benetton in the closing stages of the race.

The result was remarkable. The stands emptied almost instantly, and by the time the German driver victoriously took the chequered flag, most of the Brazilian fans were filing towards the exit gates. Three months later, those loyal enthusiasts were lining the streets of São Paulo, just as their predecessors had respectfully celebrated Emerson Fittipaldi's first World Championship triumph two decades earlier.

Williams, meanwhile, continued their winning ways. Although Schumacher's Benetton was victorious in the 1995 Brazilian GP, Damon Hill and Jacques Villeneuve ensured that Williams posted unchallenged victories at Interlagos in both 1996 and 1997.

Ferrari scored a brace of wins at Interlagos in 1976 and 1977 thanks to Niki Lauda and Carlos Reutemann, respectively. The race was then switched to Rio de Janeiro in 1978 before returning to São Paulo again for the next two years. However, the battle between Brazil's two cities for the custody of the race proved to be an on-going affair, and Rio seemed to win decisively when the race returned there in 1981 and stayed for the following eight years.

However, nothing is cut and dried in Brazilian politics and, in 1980, Interlagos reclaimed its heritage and regained possession of the country's most prestigious sporting event. By now, Ayrton Senna was riding high as the McLaren-Honda team leader and looked clear favourite to win in front of his home-town fans. Unfortunately, a brush with a slower car resulted in Senna damaging his car's nose and he was obliged to make an unscheduled pit stop – a delay that handed victory to his arch-rival Alain Prost, who had switched to the Ferrari team at the start of the season after two increasingly impossible years trying to co-exist as Senna's partner at McLaren.

The São Paulo enthusiasts pack the Interlagos grandstands from an early hour on race morning, a patient, if noisy, throng of humanity.

ARGENTINA

AUTODROMO OSCAR ALFREDO GALVEZ, BUENOS AIRES

CIRCUIT LENGTH:
2.646 miles (4.259km).
LAP RECORD:
Gerhard Berger
(3.0 Benetton-Renault B197), 1m 27.981s,
108.286mph (174.265kmph).
Lap record established in 1997.

CIRCUIT ASSESSMENT by DAVID COULTHARD:

'Quite an interesting circuit configuration, but extremely bumpy and difficult to overtake. The best chance to pass is into the sharp right-hander immediately after the pits. Otherwise, you pretty well have to rely on the guy in front making a mistake.'

ARGENTINA PLAYED A PIVOTAL ROLE IN THE EARLY YEARS OF THE OFFICIAL WORLD CHAMPIONSHIP DURING THE EARLY 1950S, WHEN TWO OF ITS FAVOURITE SONS – JUAN MANUEL FANGIO AND FROILAN GONZALEZ – WERE IN THE FOREFRONT OF FORMULA 1 COMPETITION.

Fangio, of course, would go on to win an all-time record of five World Championships before his retirement in 1958, and the sport's popularity in his native land went hand-in-hand with his rise to international prominence. In 1951, the Mercedes-Benz team had come to Argentina with three of its pre-war W154 'Silver Arrows' and Fangio had been recruited to drive one of these in the Gran Premio Presidente Perón on a makeshift road circuit in Buenos Aires's suburb of Costanera.

However, the organizers of the race had ensured that the circuit layout was sufficiently tight and tortuous so as to handicap the unwieldy supercharged Mercedes. This handed the advantage to Gonzalez, who won the race commandingly in a 2-litre Ferrari 166. Nevertheless, the race proved to be an enormously popular event in Argentina, one that gave added impetus to Perón's plans to build a purpose-made track, which was completed and ready for international racing in 1953.

Carlos Reutemann's Brabham BT34 (left) is challenged by François Cevert's Tyrrell–Ford during the 1972 Argentine Grand Prix at Buenos Aires. Reutemann never won his home race, but by 1997 he had carved out a distinguished political career.

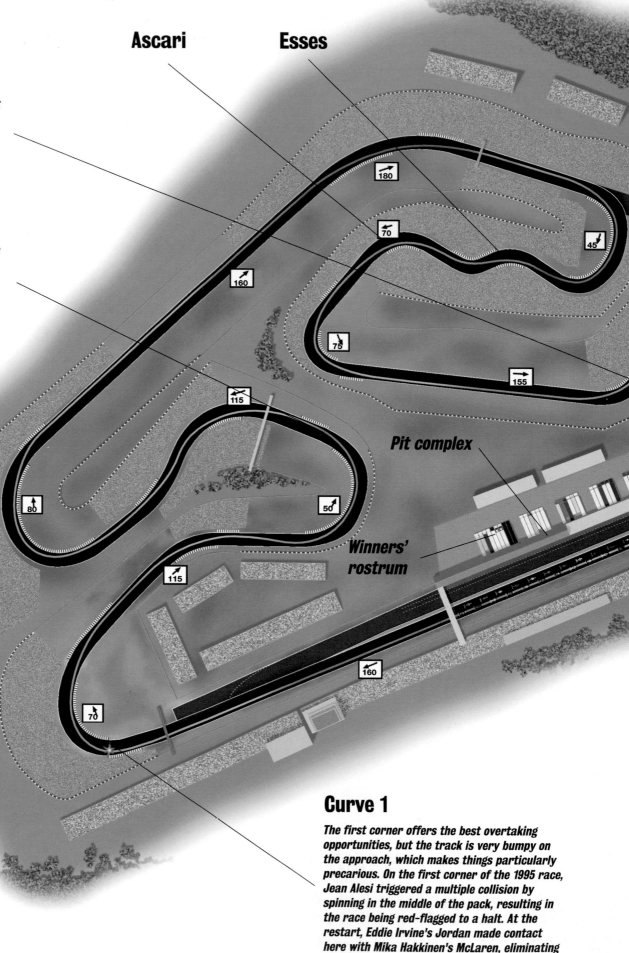

Ascari

Esses

Martin Brundle was eliminated from the 1996 race at this point when his Jordan was rammed from behind by the Minardi driven by Tarso Marques. Neither driver was injured.

Confiteria Curve

Pedro Diniz spun out of the 1996 Grand Prix at this point when his Ligier caught fire following a problem with its refuelling nozzle at a previous pit stop. The Brazilian driver escaped unhurt, but the car was quite badly damaged.

Pit complex

Winners' rostrum

Curve 1

The first corner offers the best overtaking opportunities, but the track is very bumpy on the approach, which makes things particularly precarious. On the first corner of the 1995 race, Jean Alesi triggered a multiple collision by spinning in the middle of the pack, resulting in the race being red-flagged to a halt. At the restart, Eddie Irvine's Jordan made contact here with Mika Hakkinen's McLaren, eliminating the latter, but on this occasion the race was allowed to continue.

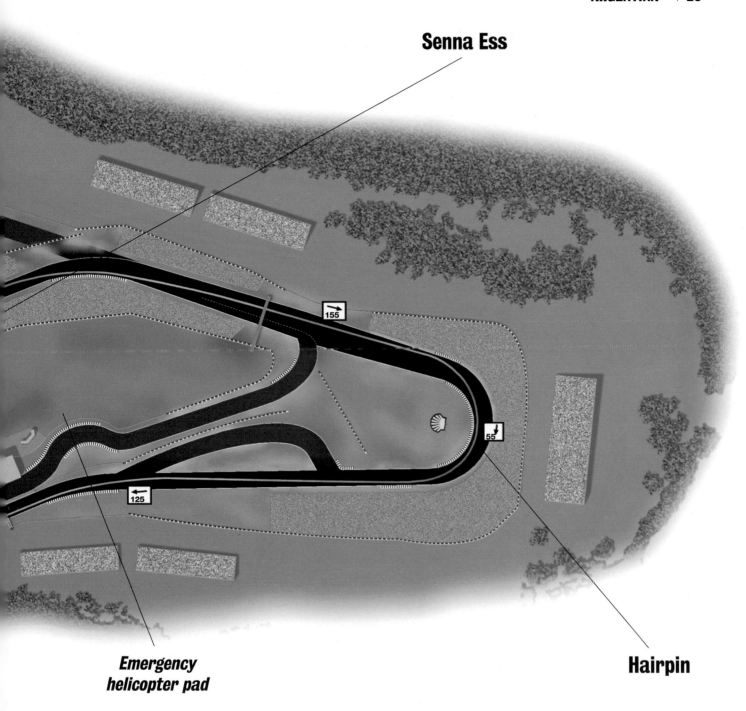

Senna Ess

155 →

← 125

55 ↓

**Emergency
helicopter pad**

Hairpin

CIRCUIT LENGTH:
2.646 miles (4.259km)

 = mph

ARGENTINIAN GRAND PRIX
AUTODROMO OSCAR ALFREDO
GALVEZ, BUENOS AIRES

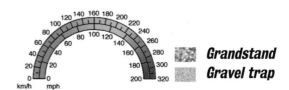

Grandstand
Gravel trap

Situated in the imposing Parc Almirante Brown on the eastern fringes of Buenos Aires, the Autodromo 17 October was duly named after a crucial date on the Perónist calendar, the day in 1947 when the future president was acclaimed by massive crowds in Buenos Aires. The circuit configuration was varied considerably over the years, with a 3.71-mile (5.97-km) length eventually adopted in the early 1970s.

The first World Championship Argentine Grand Prix took place in 1953 in conditions of utter and complete chaos. Perón's fans crammed into the circuit and broke down the frail safety fences, such as they were, the moment President Perón arrived and the troops and police, who had been drafted in for security reasons, duly stood to attention for the national anthem. By the time the race began, spectators were literally lining the very edge of the circuit. Tragedy was inevitable.

Alberto Ascari led throughout in his Ferrari, but when an over-zealous spectator ran out in front of his team-mate, Giuseppe Farina, the Italian veteran swerved and ploughed into the densely packed spectators. Nine people were killed and 40 injured.

Needless to say, spectator security was improved dramatically for the 1954 race, which was won by Fangio at the wheel of a Maserati. In 1955 he won again for Mercedes-Benz, in 1956 for Ferrari and, finally, in 1957 back in a Maserati once again.

In 1958, the Buenos Aires race yielded one of the most significant results in contemporary F1 history. Stirling Moss was contracted to drive for Tony

'YOU PRETTY WELL HAVE TO RELY ON THE GUY IN

Vandervell's Vanwall team at the time, but they opted to miss the race and the Englishman accepted an invitation to drive a rear-engined 2-litre Cooper-Climax fielded by Rob Walker, one of the sport's most celebrated private entrants.

Despite giving away around 50 horsepower to the front-engined Ferrari and Maserati opposition, Moss's delicate touch enabled the little Cooper to run non-stop without a tyre change to score an historic victory – the first for a rear-engined F1 machine in a World Championship Grand Prix.

After 1960, Argentina's political uncertainty resulted in the race being dropped from the calendar, and the elegant parkland circuit, with its wide, grassy run-off areas, was not used again for an international

race until January 1971, when Chris Amon triumphed in a non-Championship event at the wheel of a French Matra V12.

That same month saw international sports-car racing return to the Parc Almirante Brown, but this was marred by an accident that cost the life of works Ferrari driver Ignazio Giunti, who collided with the crippled Matra sports car that Jean-Pierre Beltoise was pushing back to the pits along the short straight from the hairpin adjacent to the park gates.

This disaster resulted in the circuit being altered to incorporate a tighter, earlier hairpin immediately before the pits, a section of the track that remains largely unchanged to this day. World Championship F1 racing returned to Buenos Aires the following

FRONT MAKING A MISTAKE'

year when Carlos Reutemann, the country's then rising star, qualified on pole position at the wheel of a Brabham-Ford.

Reutemann's emergence as a world-class driver through the 1970s guaranteed the race a permanent place on the F1 calendar, even though political problems caused it to miss a year in 1976. However, the gifted driver from Santa Fe province was never quite able to deliver the home victory his fans so desperately yearned for. In 1974, Reutemann dominated the event at the wheel of a works Brabham-Ford, only to run out of fuel in the closing moments. This was due to a dire miscalculation by the team's mechanics, who had failed to put sufficient fuel in the car before the start of the race.

By 1974 Perón had returned from exile to retake the presidency, and the ailing dictator, only a few months from his death, attended the race where Reutemann was duly fêted despite his bitter disappointment. Carlos's best result in front of his home crowd was second in 1981 in a Williams, after which the race was again dropped from the calendar. Reutemann retired from driving early the following year.

For 1995 the race was restored to the calendar, but on a very truncated 2.646-mile (4.259-km) circuit, which was a mere shadow of the track's former self. Since then, Williams have remained unbeaten in Argentina, with Damon Hill winning the race in both 1995 and 1996 while Jacques Villeneuve continued the tradition in 1997, although it was a close call for the Canadian driver, since eddie Irvine's Ferrari was less than a second behind at the chequered flag.

The Buenos Aires infield section during the 1996 Argentine Grand Prix. The circuit's characteristically wide run-off areas were retained when the circuit was reintroduced to the F1 calendar in 1995.

AUTODROMO DINO E ENZO FERRARI, IMOLA

CIRCUIT LENGTH FROM 1997: 3.063 miles (4.930km).
LAP RECORD: Heinz-Harald Frentzen
(3.0 Williams-Renault FW19), 1m 25.531s,
128.936mph (207.496kmph).
Lap record established in 1997.

CIRCUIT ASSESSMENT by DAMON HILL:

'Obviously a track with emotional memories for those of us who were there in 1994 when Ayrton was killed. It used to be quite a good circuit to judge a car by, but since it has been broken up by those two new chicanes, I think it has less of a rhythm to it. You have to hustle the car pretty hard now.'

Like Hockenheim, the emotionally titled Autodromo Dino e Enzo Ferrari at Imola, just off the *Autostrada* between Bologna and Rimini, will be damned in the eyes of motor-racing enthusiasts for ever. Just as the German circuit claimed the life of the legendary Jim Clark, so 26 years and 24 days later, Imola was the scene of the fatal accident involving Ayrton Senna, when his Williams FW14 crashed at high speed while leading the seventh lap of the San Marino Grand Prix.

Unlike Clark's accident, in which the moment of impact was not witnessed by a soul, the Senna tragedy unfolded live across the world on prime-time television. It served as a poignant reminder of just how far the sport had progressed in just over a generation, from a position as an admittedly extremely popular minority interest to one of the biggest global television festivals of the century.

It was all a far cry from the day in 1948, when some local enthusiasts envisaged the construction of a permanent race track at Imola as part of the Italian

Nicola Larini's Ferrari sweeps through the S-bends before the start/finish area at Imola on its way to second place behind Schumacher's Benetton in the 1994 San Marino Grand Prix.

SAN MARINO GRAND PRIX AUTODROMO DINO E ENZO FERRARI, IMOLA

CIRCUIT LENGTH:
3.063 miles (4.930km)

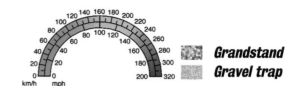

Grandstand
Gravel trap

= mph

Ayrton Senna ended up taking a surprise trip into this gravel trap while leading the 1989 race. A problem with a damaged rear wheel rim caused his McLaren to develop a slow puncture, leading to his premature departure from the race.

Variante Alta

Michael Andretti spun off here in his McLaren-Ford while running in the top six during the 1993 race. It was another major setback for the Indycar ace and a slip that contributed to his being dropped by the team before the end of the year.

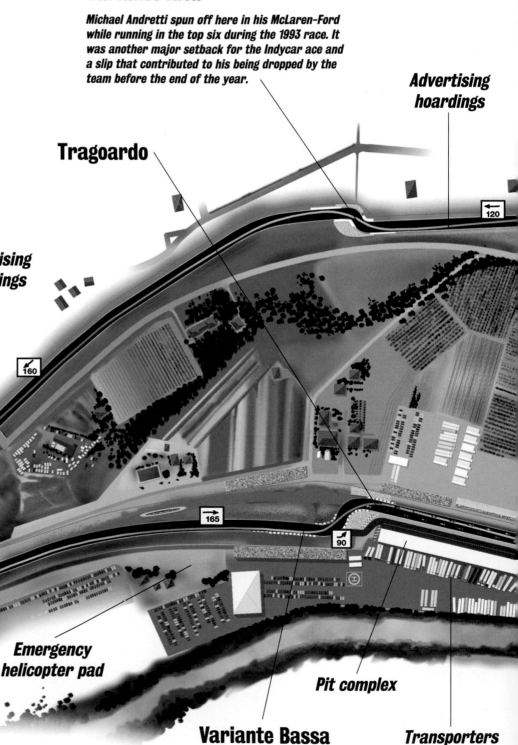

Advertising hoardings

Tragoardo

Advertising hoardings

Rivazza

Emergency helicopter pad

Variante Bassa

Pit complex

Transporters

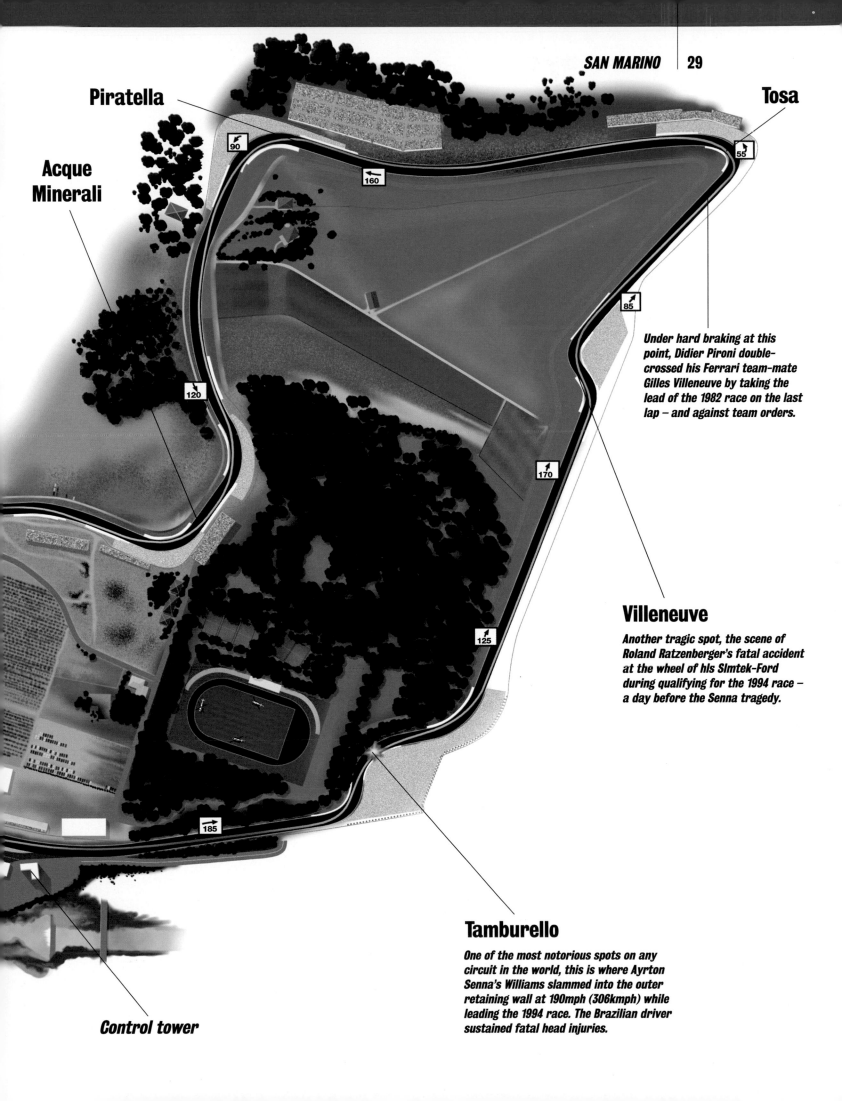

Piratella

**Acque
Minerali**

Tosa

Villeneuve

Another tragic spot, the scene of
Roland Ratzenberger's fatal accident
at the wheel of his Simtek-Ford
during qualifying for the 1994 race –
a day before the Senna tragedy.

Under hard braking at this
point, Didier Pironi double-
crossed his Ferrari team-mate
Gilles Villeneuve by taking the
lead of the 1982 race on the last
lap – and against team orders.

Tamburello

One of the most notorious spots on any
circuit in the world, this is where Ayrton
Senna's Williams slammed into the outer
retaining wall at 190mph (306kmph) while
leading the 1994 race. The Brazilian driver
sustained fatal head injuries.

Control tower

Moments before Ayrton Senna's fatal accident in the opening laps of the 1994 San Marino Grand Prix, the Brazilian driver's Williams leads Michael Schumacher's Benetton, Gerhard Berger's Ferrari and Damon Hill's Williams. They are seen here braking for the uphill left-hander at Tosa.

'I THINK IT HAS LESS OF A RHYTHM TO IT.

Olympic Committee's grandiose plans to build as many as 12 circuits in Italy. Building eventually started in 1950, with the circuit being officially opened in 1952 when Giuseppe Farina, Formula 1's first official World Champion, drove around the circuit in a Ferrari sports car.

The 3.11-mile (5-km) track more closely resembled a network of public roads laid out on the edge of the town, rising and diving a spectacular path through vineyards and open countryside. It was one of those circuits on which a driver could get into a comfortable rhythm, with long flowing corners that were immensely satisfying to drive.

However, although Imola hosted a number of sports-car races during the 1950s, it was primarily as a motorcycle venue that it came to be known. In that connection, it was also the track on which the talented southern Rhodesian rider Ray Amm crashed and died in April 1955, giving his all in one of the Italian factory MV Agustas.

Not until 1963 did Imola host its first F1 race – a non-Championship event contested by the works Lotus entries of Jim Clark and Trevor Taylor, but not,

disappointingly, by any works Ferraris. The Italian home team had withdrawn its entries for former motorcycle ace John Surtees and his team-mate Willy Mairesse on the grounds that the cars were not ready. More likely, Ferrari did not wish to risk a public drubbing on his home ground. Clark duly won at a canter, at an average speed of over 90mph (145kmph), after Taylor encountered gear-change problems.

Thereafter, Imola settled down to a diet of sports-car and European Championship F2 events until 1979, when the grandly titled Grand Premio Dino Ferrari di F1 was held. This was just a week after South African driver Jody Scheckter had clinched the World Championship for Ferrari with an unchallenged victory in the Italian Grand Prix at Monza.

This one-off event was eventually won by Niki Lauda's Brabham-Alfa Romeo, serving as a curtain-raiser for Imola to host the Italian Grand Prix as a one-off arrangement in 1980. The track authorities complied with requests for major circuit changes, most notably the inclusion of an S-bend complex before the start/finish line and the slowing of the plunging Acque Minerali corner on the return leg of

The Renaults of René Arnoux and Alain Prost lead the Ferraris of Gilles Villeneuve and Didier Pironi away from the Imola grid at the start of the controversial 1982 San Marino Grand Prix.

YOU HAVE TO HUSTLE THE CAR PRETTY HARD NOW'

the circuit by reshaping it into a first-gear chicane that most drivers agreed was absurdly tight.

The 1980 Italian Grand Prix was a largely unmemorable affair, with Nelson Piquet's Brabham BT49 dominating the event ahead of the Williams FW07s of Alan Jones and Carlos Reutemann. Ferrari star Gilles Villeneuve escaped substantially unhurt from a 170-mph (274-kmph) crash on the approach to the Tosa hairpin when one of his rear tyres exploded. He was taken to the medical centre for a checkup after which he was released, bruised and shaken, but otherwise none the worse for his escapade.

Appropriately enough, considering the circuit's official title, Imola witnessed an all-Ferrari battle for victory in the 1982 San Marino Grand Prix after the race fell victim to a boycott by the predominantly British-based rival F1 teams aligned to the powerful Formula One Constructors' Association. This had been prompted by a battle for power between the FOCA team owners and the sport's governing body, the FIA. Ostensibly, this was about who had the power to make and interpret the complex technical and sporting rules that governed the sport. Beneath

the surface, however, the dispute also concerned the far wider-reaching implications of who controlled the television income that was beginning to become a major element within the F1 business.

The bottom line was that the British teams stayed away from the race to signal their disapproval of an FIA edict concerning particular technical regulations, and the result was that only nine cars lined up on the Imola starting grid. Despite this, the pulling power of Ferrari among Italian fans was amply demonstrated when they attended *en masse* and were treated to a spellbinding internecine battle between Gilles Villeneuve and Didier Pironi.

In the end, Pironi slipstreamed past to win going into the final lap, but he had overtaken Villeneuve against Ferrari team orders and the day ended with considerable bad feeling between the two men. Only 13 days later, Villeneuve would crash fatally trying to beat Pironi's lap time during practice for the Belgian Grand Prix at Zolder.

Although Italy had lost one of its sporting heroes, thankfully the San Marino Grand Prix continued to prosper throughout the 1980s and beyond, becoming one of the most popular races on the F1 calendar. The crowd was always extremely good natured, even if access to the track seemed utterly chaotic, in particular for those approaching from Bologna via the *autostrada*. The last mile or so to the circuit gates is often impossible no matter which direction they are approached from, so the best option is to park at the roadside and walk the final section.

One area of continuing concern, however, was the daunting Tamburello left-hander beyond the pits. Since the early 1980s this was easily negotiated flat-out in the contemporary breed of high-downforce Grand Prix machine, but, in effect, the driver was just a passenger on this section of the circuit. If anything went wrong, the outcome could be disastrous.

The potential for a huge accident at Tamburello was finally realized in 1989 when Gerhard Berger's Ferrari lost part of its nose wing while in seventh position in the early stages of the race. Deprived of aerodynamic downforce on its front wheels, Berger's car slid wide at 170mph (275kmph) going into the fast left-hander and slammed into the retaining wall.

After skidding along the wall for several hundred metres the Ferrari burst into flames. Rescue vehicles were, thankfully, on the scene in seconds, extinguishing the conflagration in textbook style. Berger survived with a few broken bones and burns and was back in the cockpit a couple of races later. But the warning signs were not heeded in terms of Imola's circuit safety.

Ironically, the 1989 race saw another Villeneuve/Pironi-style confrontation when Alain Prost accused his McLaren-Honda team-mate Ayrton Senna of reneging on a no-passing agreement on the first lap of the restart. It was an episode that caused a great deal of rancour between these two Formula 1 aces

Senna's Williams leads the pack behind the pace car in the early stages of the 1994 San Marino Grand Prix, which ended with his tragically fatal accident.

and aggravated the discord that eventually saw Prost leave the team at the end of the season.

Finally, in 1994, the Imola circuit would be visited by a double tragedy of absolutely catastrophic proportions. During Saturday qualifying, the Austrian novice Roland Ratzenberger was killed in a violent 190-mph (306-kmph) accident when his Simtek-Ford suffered a structural failure approaching Tosa on the fastest part of the track.

The following day, Ayrton Senna's Williams-Renault plunged off the track at Tamburello while leading the San Marino Grand Prix, and the

Jacques Villeneuve's Williams is elbowed on to the grass in the first-lap scramble during the 1996 San Marino Grand Prix. The pack is exiting the Villeneuve chicane, so named after Jacques's father, Gilles, who escaped a huge accident at this point during the 1980 race.

Brazilian driver suffered major head injuries to which he succumbed later that day. By the time the F1 teams returned to the Autodromo Dino e Enzo Ferrari in 1995, the circuit had been further changed, almost beyond recognition.

At both Tamburello and on the approach to Tosa, there were now medium-speed chicanes designed to slow the cars down. Acque Minerali had also been slowed, as had the Piratella left-hander at the top of the hill beyond Tosa. There is no doubt that Imola was still an occasion, reflecting the Italians' great passion for motor racing, but in terms of a racing venue it was now, sadly and considerably, much reduced in terms of driver appeal.

In particular, the exit from Tamburello and the approach to Tosa had presented classic, high-speed overtaking opportunities, with F1 cars building up to about 180mph (290kmph) before darting out of their rivals' slipstreams. New Williams team recruit Heinz-Harald Frentzen proved he had the skill to tackle the revised circuit with a superbly well-judged victory over Schumacher in 1997. It was the first time in the history of the World Championship that German drivers finished the race in first and second places.

MONACO

CIRCUIT DE MONACO

CIRCUIT LENGTH FROM 1997:
2.092 miles (3.366km).
LAP RECORD:
Michael Schumacher
(3.0 Ferrari F310B), 1m 53.315s,
66.447mph (106.937kmph).
Lap record established in 1997 (during wet race).

CIRCUIT ASSESSMENT by ALAIN PROST:

'This is regarded as the classic Grand Prix circuit on the Championship programme and it is a track where absolute precision and consistency reap dividends. If you are impulsive at Monaco, you are likely to end up in the barrier. Overtaking is extremely difficult and opportunities to do so seldom present themselves. It can be enormously frustrating, but, equally, very satisfying.'

THE MONACO GRAND PRIX HAS LONG BEEN REGARDED AS THE JEWEL IN F1 RACING'S INTERNATIONAL CROWN, EVEN THOUGH MOST COMPETITORS REGARD THE CHASE THROUGH THE STREETS AS NOTHING MORE THAN AN EXERCISE IN PRECISION HIGH-SPEED DRIVING. IN TERMS OF PURE RACING, MONACO IS ONE OF THE MOST DIFFICULT CIRCUITS ON WHICH TO OVERTAKE, YET THAT UNDERLYING FACT IN NO WAY COMPROMISES ITS POSITION AS ONE OF THE MOST MAGNETICALLY POPULAR EVENTS ON THE WORLD CHAMPIONSHIP CALENDAR.

The race was the brainchild of Antony Noghes, Founder-President of the Automobile Club de Monaco, and the man who worked out the obvious route for a possible race in 1928. Noghes had quite a fight to sell the idea of such an event to those who controlled the principality's levers of power, but he pulled it off and the continued existence of the race stands as a tribute to his tenacity and determination.

Michael Schumacher's Ferrari F310 locks over hard into the Loews hairpin at Monaco during practice for the 1996 Grand Prix.

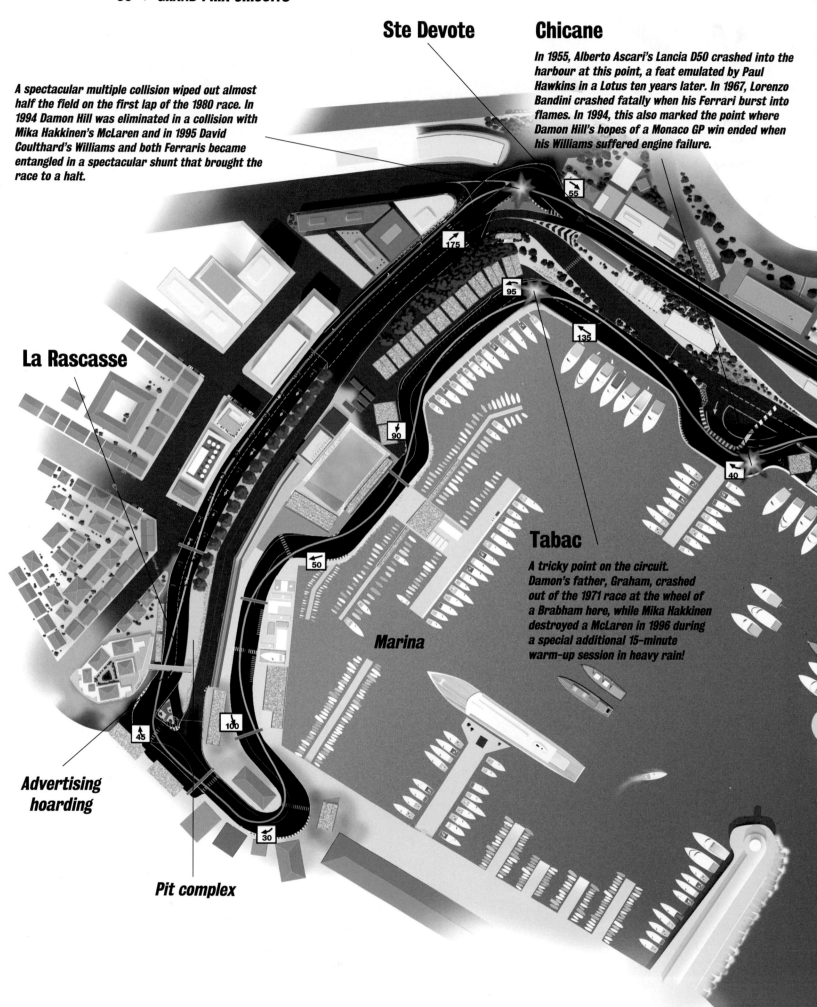

Ste Devote

A spectacular multiple collision wiped out almost half the field on the first lap of the 1980 race. In 1994 Damon Hill was eliminated in a collision with Mika Hakkinen's McLaren and in 1995 David Coulthard's Williams and both Ferraris became entangled in a spectacular shunt that brought the race to a halt.

Chicane

In 1955, Alberto Ascari's Lancia D50 crashed into the harbour at this point, a feat emulated by Paul Hawkins in a Lotus ten years later. In 1967, Lorenzo Bandini crashed fatally when his Ferrari burst into flames. In 1994, this also marked the point where Damon Hill's hopes of a Monaco GP win ended when his Williams suffered engine failure.

La Rascasse

Tabac

A tricky point on the circuit. Damon's father, Graham, crashed out of the 1971 race at the wheel of a Brabham here, while Mika Hakkinen destroyed a McLaren in 1996 during a special additional 15-minute warm-up session in heavy rain!

Marina

Advertising hoarding

Pit complex

175

55

95

135

90

50

40

100

45

30

MONACO GRAND PRIX CIRCUIT DE MONACO

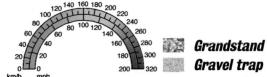

Grandstand
Gravel trap

CIRCUIT LENGTH:
2.092 miles (3.366km)

☐ = mph

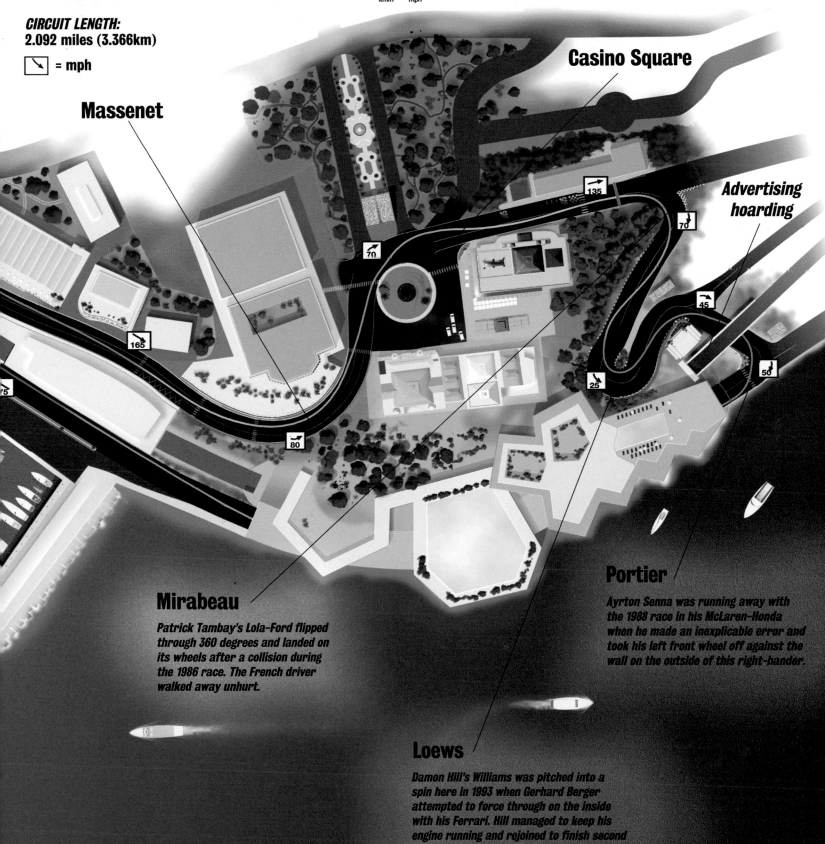

Massenet

Casino Square

Advertising hoarding

Mirabeau

Patrick Tambay's Lola-Ford flipped
through 360 degrees and landed on
its wheels after a collision during
the 1986 race. The French driver
walked away unhurt.

Portier

Ayrton Senna was running away with
the 1988 race in his McLaren-Honda
when he made an inexplicable error and
took his left front wheel off against the
wall on the outside of this right-hander.

Loews

Damon Hill's Williams was pitched into a
spin here in 1993 when Gerhard Berger
attempted to force through on the inside
with his Ferrari. Hill managed to keep his
engine running and rejoined to finish second
behind Senna's McLaren, but Berger was out
on the spot with broken suspension.

Ayrton Senna's McLaren-Honda hurtles up the hill beyond Ste Devote on the approach to Massenet. The brilliant Brazilian won at Monaco a record six times – once for Lotus, five times at the wheel of a McLaren.

Monaco hosted its first 'Grand Prix' back in 1929 when the enigmatically named 'Williams' won at the wheel of his Bugatti. This was a pseudonym for William Grover-Williams, a *dégagé* sportsman who later died during the Second World War while operating as a British agent in occupied France. In those days, of course, Monaco was a refined, if conservative, Mediterranean backwater, a far cry from the glitzy tax haven for the rich and famous that it subsequently became.

René Dreyfus and Louis Chiron won the race in 1930 and 1931 to score a Bugatti hat-trick, but then Alfa Romeo entered the equation with wins in 1932 and 1934, thanks to the efforts of Tazio Nuvolari and Guy Moll. Subsequently, the Nazi-backed Mercedes works team scored a hat-trick of wins before the race lapsed in 1938 due to financial and political problems. It was staged again in 1948, then skipped a year to be revived in the first year of the official World Championship, when Juan Manuel Fangio emerged as the winner driving an Alfa Romeo.

With the Monte Carlo topography firmly dictating the route taken by this demanding street race, the track layout understandably changed little over the years. The start line was originally positioned on the harbour front, presenting competitors with a short sprint into a tight, right-hand hairpin. Only after a multiple collision in 1962, in which a marshal was killed by a flying wheel, did the organizers see fit to reposition the start line on the other side of the hairpin, where it remains to this day.

The first corner, Ste Devote, is a tricky uphill right-hander followed by a long climb up to Casino Square, the cars bursting through a fast left-hander in front of the elegant Hotel de Paris before slamming over a brow and plunging down to what was originally called Station Hairpin. However, the railway's path through Monaco was re-sited during the 1970s and the pricy Loews Hotel now occupies this prime site, there being no apparent shortage of guests prepared to pay the earth for a view of the racing action.

Thereafter, the track wends back to the edge of the sea, before plunging through a tunnel, back through what was originally a dauntingly fast chicane – now slowed considerably – and back towards the original harbour front. In 1973, this section was dramatically reshaped on a section of land reclaimed from the sea, and the cars now zigzag through a very tight section around the swimming pool before rejoining the original track layout on the exit of the final hairpin.

'IF YOU ARE IMPULSIVE AT MONACO, YOU

Monaco's tight waterfront chicane in its current guise. It was here that Alberto Ascari (1955) and Paul Hawkins (1965) ended up in the harbour and Lorenzo Bandini was fatally injured in 1967.

The nature of the Monaco circuit always put an absolute premium on driver skill. Many times in its history, outstanding competitors in below-par machinery have taken their rivals to the cleaners, most notably in 1961 when Stirling Moss used his underpowered, four-cylinder Rob Walker team Lotus 18 to defeat the might of the Ferrari works team, which had the benefit of far more powerful cars. Phil Hill, who finished third that year for Ferrari, commented that chasing Moss in those circumstances was 'like a cart horse chasing a greyhound round somebody's living room!'

Yet despite the fact that it had one of the slowest lap speeds on the Formula 1 calendar, Monaco could bite the unwary. In 1955, Alberto Ascari's Lancia D50 locked a brake on the approach to the chicane.

The Italian car and driver slewed across the road, burst through the straw bales and catapulted into the harbour. Ascari quickly bobbed to the surface and struck out strongly for a nearby rescue boat. Poignantly, having survived this close shave, the legendary Italian was killed less than a week later while testing a Ferrari sports car at Monza.

Ten years later, Aussie Paul Hawkins duplicated Ascari's escapade and emerged unhurt after another unscheduled immersion, but in 1967 the Monaco Grand Prix produced a horrifying accident that pushed the issue of safety and security to the forefront of the F1 agenda.

Chasing Denny Hulme's winning Brabham in the closing stages of the race, Ferrari driver Lorenzo Bandini clipped the inside kerb at the chicane and

ARE LIKELY TO END UP IN THE BARRIER'

was launched into the straw bales on the opposite side of the circuit. The car flipped over and burst into flames. Bandini, fatally injured, was eventually extricated from the wreckage, but the whole grisly episode was played out in front of the world's television cameras. Today, the race would have been stopped instantly in such circumstances, but 30 years ago things were different and events were permitted to run their course.

On a happier note, Graham Hill scored the first hat-trick of Monaco wins between 1963 and 1965, adding further wins in 1968 and 1969 to set a record only beaten when Ayrton Senna won the race for the sixth time in 1993. Ironically, Hill's son, Damon, has yet to match his father's achievement with a win at Monaco, even though he led commandingly throughout the 1995 race before his bid was thwarted by engine failure.

In many ways, Monaco is an anachronism in a safety-orientated age. If such a track configuration was laid down at any other venue, it is unlikely anybody would even consider racing on it.

Overtaking opportunities at Circuit de Monaco depend largely on the cooperation of the car in front and they are achieved mainly under hard braking for the waterfront chicane, although the audacious may attempt a passing move either at Ste Devote – the right-hander after the start – or, conceivably, under braking for the Mirabeau right-hander on the plunge down out of Casino Square.

This confined and slightly claustrophobic-feeling environment also means that it is very difficult to lap a slower car unless the driver concerned is feeling in a cooperative frame of mind. The track is particularly narrow at both the Loews Hotel hairpin and on the waterfront section around the swimming pool, so any driver prepared to take huge risks by passing backmarkers can gain a considerable advantage.

In this respect, the late Ayrton Senna was a master at Monaco. The very presence of his bright yellow helmet in any driver's rear-view mirror was sufficient to guarantee him safe passage past a slower car, such was the intensity of his intimidating presence.

In the three years since Senna's death, Michael Schumacher has unquestionably taken over his mantle as F1's top performer. His dominant victory in the rain-soaked Monaco Grand Prix was one of the very best of his entire career.

In primitive surroundings, Graham Hill's Lotus 49B swings into Tabac en route to victory in the 1968 Monaco Grand Prix. Note the absence of guard rails protecting the edge of the harbourfront!

CIRCUIT DE CATALUNYA, BARCELONA

CIRCUIT LENGTH:
2.936 miles (4.725km).
LAP RECORD:
Giancarlo Fisichella
(3.0 Jordan-Peugeot 197), 1m 22.242s,
128.604mph (206.968kmph).
Lap record established in 1997.

CIRCUIT ASSESSMENT by GERHARD BERGER:

'This is a good example of how to build a new Grand Prix circuit, offering lots of variety and good corners. It also has a long straight leading into a medium-speed corner, which has proved, time and again, to offer scope for lots of overtaking.'

SPAIN'S F1 WORLD CHAMPIONSHIP QUALIFYING RACE HAS LED A SOMEWHAT NOMADIC AND TRUNCATED EXISTENCE SINCE THE FIRST OFFICIAL GRAND PRIX WAS HELD ON BARCELONA'S NOW-DEFUNCT PEDRALBES CIRCUIT IN 1951. THE FIXTURE WAS REPEATED IN 1954, BUT THE RACE THEN LAPSED FOR 14 YEARS BEFORE BEING REVIVED ON THE UNINSPIRING AND TORTUOUS JARAMA TRACK ON THE OUTSKIRTS OF MADRID.

The following year the Spanish Grand Prix moved to the spectacular Montjuich Park circuit in the centre of Barcelona, where it alternated with Jarama through to 1975 when a tragic accident cost the lives of four onlookers. The Montjuich circuit was then abandoned permanently for Formula 1 competition. Jarama survived through to 1981, however, when Spanish Grand Prix history suffered another interruption and the race was next held at the brand new Jerez de la Frontera circuit in 1986.

In 1991, the race finally arrived at its current home, the Circuit de Catalunya at Montmelo, situated on the northern fringes of Barcelona. It had originally been intended that the new circuit would not be ready until 1992 – the year in which Barcelona would host the Olympic Games – but political forces had been at work, with the result that

The McLaren-Hondas of Gerhard Berger and Ayrton Senna sprint for the first corner ahead of Nigel Mansell's Williams and the rest of the pack at the start of the 1991 Spanish Grand Prix. Mansell went on to win the race after a wheel-to-wheel battle with Senna.

SPANISH GRAND PRIX CIRCUIT DE CATALUNYA, BARCELONA

CIRCUIT LENGTH:
2.936 miles (4.725km)

↘ = mph

120 140 160 180 200
100 220
80 240
60 260
40 280
20 300
km/h mph 320

Grandstand
Gravel trap

Campsa

140

Repsol

75

140

Seat

Emergency helicopter pad

140

50

Renault

105

180

Winners' rostrum

Elf

The point where Nigel Mansell's Williams finally overtook Ayrton Senna's McLaren for the lead after a great battle in 1991.

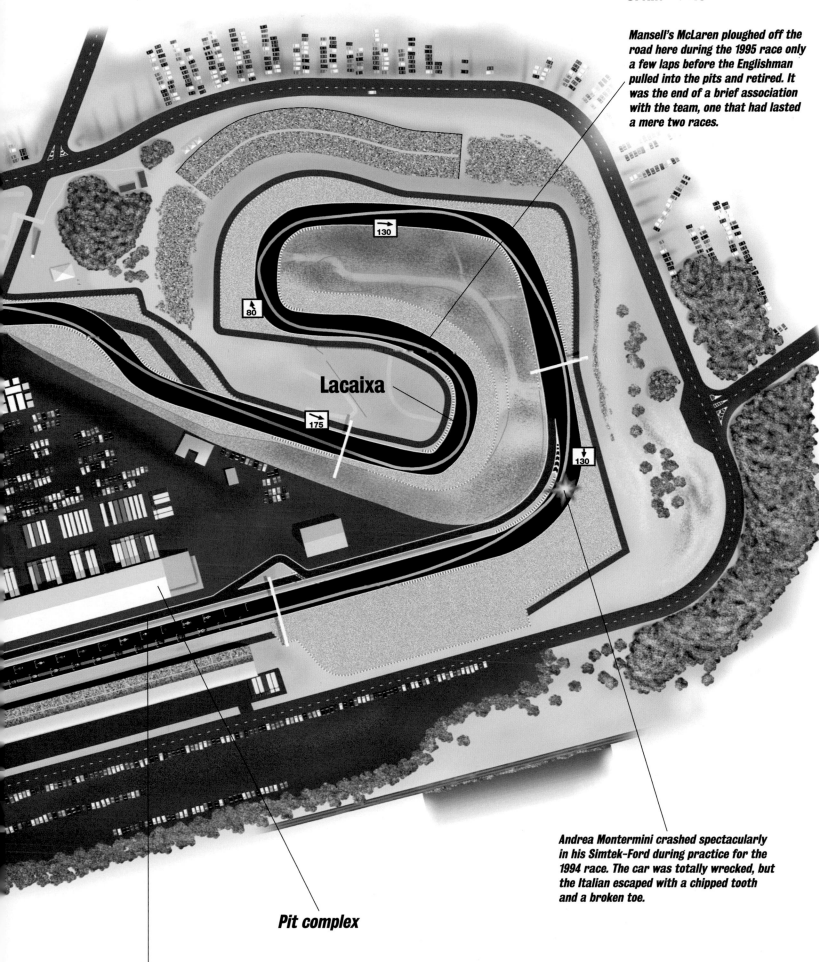

Mansell's McLaren ploughed off the road here during the 1995 race only a few laps before the Englishman pulled into the pits and retired. It was the end of a brief association with the team, one that had lasted a mere two races.

Lacaixa

Andrea Montermini crashed spectacularly in his Simtek-Ford during practice for the 1994 race. The car was totally wrecked, but the Italian escaped with a chipped tooth and a broken toe.

Pit complex

Retaining wall

The fast S-bend beyond the pits at the Circuit de Catalunya offers spectacular viewing and the possibility of close-fought overtaking moves.

international championship. Yet the drivers' verdict was instantly favourable. As new circuits go, it was impressive and highly enjoyable to drive. It offered plenty of variation, with undulations and fast corners combined with that vital ingredient for overtaking – a sweeping downhill curve leading on to a long main straight, which had a tight corner at the end of it. This is where much of the passing has always taken place.

The first Spanish Grand Prix to be held at the Circuit de Catalunya has gone down in F1 history books as one of Nigel Mansell's greatest single drives. He came into the 14th of the 16-round World Championship contest trailing Ayrton Senna by 24 points in the title battle. But he vowed to keep fighting right to the very end. And a close fight it proved to be.

Nigel Mansell won this race brilliantly, sitting it out with Senna inches apart at over 170mph (275kmph) as they raced down the start/finish straight in the early stages of the contest. It was a strategically complex race, starting with the field running on deep-grooved rain tyres, but then having to make critically astute judgements as to the timing of pit stops to change back on to dry weather slicks. In the end, Mansell crossed the line nine seconds ahead of Alain Prost's Ferrari, with Senna, delayed by a spin, trailing home fifth in his McLaren.

In 1992, Mansell repeated his Spanish success in conditions of streaming rain, this victory being one of the highlights of his personal World Championship year, while the following year's Barcelona race developed into an all-Williams confrontation between Alain Prost and Damon Hill. The

the promoters had been persuaded to have the new race track ready for Grand Prix competition a full 12 months ahead of schedule.

This seemed a tall order when the Formula 1 teams arrived for the first race in late October 1991. Sure enough, the 3.641-mile (5.859-km) circuit was indeed completed, but the paddock and surrounding areas more closely resembled a building site than a venue for a round of the sport's most prestigious

Frenchman won commandingly in the end, but only after Hill's Renault engine failed while he was challenging for the lead. Alain subsequently admitted that Damon's retirement was a lucky break.

In 1994, the Spanish Grand Prix took place in a cloud of gloom only four weeks after Ayrton Senna's fatal accident in the San Marino Grand Prix at Imola. The FIA, motor racing's governing body, had decreed that short-term technical changes should be made to reduce the speed of the competing cars. This almost resulted in the race being boycotted by several of the leading competing teams, but while the issue was eventually resolved, it tended to mask serious concerns about temporary modifications that had been made to the circuit.

In particular, the drivers were deeply worried about a makeshift chicane that had been installed on their request to slow the 150-mph (241-kmph) approach to the fast right-hand Nissan curve. This amounted to nothing more than two piles of tyres lashed together to form barriers across the track, and it should have come as no surprise that the FIA quickly reminded the circuit owners that they required official approval for insurance purposes in the event of such alterations being made.

'I know it is not ideal, but it is the best that could be arranged in the time available,' explained retired World Champion Niki Lauda, speaking on behalf of the Grand Prix Drivers' Association. 'It's certainly better than hitting a concrete wall at 300kmph!'

Thankfully, the race passed off without further incident and Damon Hill returned Williams to the winner's rostrum with a timely victory that served as a considerable morale-booster after the sadness of Imola. The following year of 1995 saw the circuit extensively reshaped in time for the event, with a new straight bypassing the Nissan curve altogether. This, in turn, made the approach to the Caixa left-hander a significantly more challenging manoeuvre, as well as providing another overtaking opportunity.

The 1995 race also marked Nigel Mansell's apparent F1 swansong after he had signed to drive for the McLaren-Mercedes team at the start of the season, while in 1996 the race took place in conditions of consistent torrential rain to yield a brilliant victory for Michael Schumacher – his first at the wheel of a Ferrari.

Schumacher had no such luck when he returned to Barcelona in 1997 in a race where most Goodyear-shod competitors had severe tyre-wear problems. The only exception was winner Jacques Villeneuve who was able to build up a comfortable early lead to conserve his Williams's rubber. Michael Schumacher trailed home in fourth position.

Jacques Villeneuve's Williams speeds past an abandoned Minardi on its way to a strong third place in the rain-soaked 1996 Spanish Grand Prix.

CANADA

CIRCUIT GILLES VILLENEUVE, MONTREAL

CIRCUIT LENGTH: 2.747 miles (4.421km).
LAP RECORD: David Coulthard (3.0 McLaren-Mercedes MP4/12), 1m 19.635s, 124.18mph (199.856kmph). Lap record established in 1997.

CIRCUIT ASSESSMENT by EDDIE IRVINE:

'This always keeps you extremely busy. With two hairpins per lap, it is understandably hard on the tyres and brakes and has a wide variety of other corners as well. It is very rewarding to drive when everything clicks together.'

CANADA'S FIRST WORLD CHAMPIONSHIP GRAND PRIX TOOK PLACE AT THE MOSPORT PARK CIRCUIT, NEAR TORONTO, IN 1967. IT THEN BRIEFLY ALTERNATED WITH THE CIRCUIT MONT TREMBLANT UP UNTIL 1970 WHEN THIS SPLENDID TRACK NEAR MONTREAL CLOSED ITS DOORS TO INTERNATIONAL COMPETITION.

After the closure of Circuit Mont Tremblant the race reverted to Mosport, where it remained until 1977, apart from a break in 1975 due to financial problems. However, the rise of French-Canadian star Gilles Villeneuve as an F1 force prompted its switch to the Circuit Ile Notre Dame on the St Lawrence River, not far from downtown Montreal.

The track was laid out around the perimeter of an island within the complex originally built for the Expo '67 exhibition, adjacent to the artificial lake that was used for rowing competitions during the 1968 Olympic Games. It proved to be one of the most easily accessible tracks on the World Championship trail, a short subway ride from Montreal's city centre.

The Canadian Grand Prix was first held there as the final round of the 1978 World Championship battle and produced a fairy tale result, with Gilles Villeneuve winning at the wheel of his Ferrari in

Johnny Herbert's Sauber-Ford accelerating hard down the return straight at Montreal, passing the site of the old, original pit complex, which was moved prior to the 1988 race.

CANADIAN GRAND PRIX CIRCUIT GILLES VILLENEUVE, MONTREAL

CIRCUIT LENGTH:
2.747 miles (4.421km)

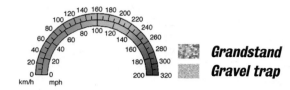

Grandstand
Gravel trap

☒ = mph

This was where David Coulthard's Williams ended up after spinning off on the second lap of the 1995 race – before which he was running ahead of the eventual winner, Jean Alesi.

The scene of many great overtaking manoeuvres, most notably when Alan Jones overtook Gilles Villeneuve for the lead of the 1979 race and Ayrton Senna did the same to Alain Prost nine years later. In 1995, Mika Hakkinen contrived to T-bone Johnny Herbert in a less successful effort.

Virage Du Casino

180

170

170

35

Bridge

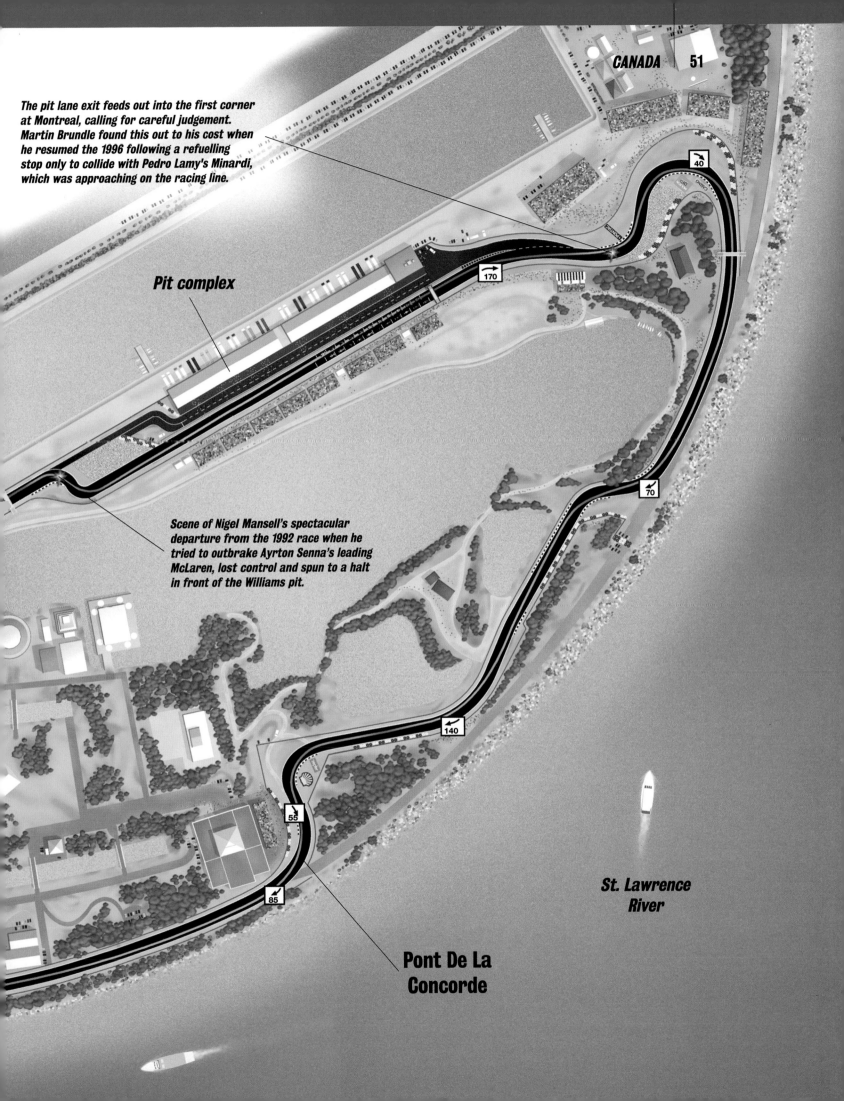

The pit lane exit feeds out into the first corner at Montreal, calling for careful judgement. Martin Brundle found this out to his cost when he resumed the 1996 following a refuelling stop only to collide with Pedro Lamy's Minardi, which was approaching on the racing line.

Pit complex

Scene of Nigel Mansell's spectacular departure from the 1992 race when he tried to outbrake Ayrton Senna's leading McLaren, lost control and spun to a halt in front of the Williams pit.

40

170

70

140

55

85

Pont De La Concorde

St. Lawrence River

'IT IS VERY REWARDING TO DRIVE WHEN

front of an excited capacity crowd, which included the country's Prime Minister Pierre Trudeau.

From the outset, the Ile Notre Dame track was greeted in a positive spirit by the drivers. With two tight hairpins at either end, linked by a series of medium-speed and fast swerves, it offered plenty of overtaking opportunities, even though the run-off areas were distinctly limited. Initially, the pit facilities were open to the elements and were of a makeshift nature, but a totally new complex was erected further down the circuit in time for the 1988 race.

Villeneuve's presence was the catalyst that ensured the race's popularity for the first few years. In 1979, the dauntless French Canadian finished a close second to Alan Jones's Williams after a tough race-long battle, while in 1980 Villeneuve drove brilliantly through to finish fifth after starting from the back of the grid and followed that up with a strong third place in 1981.

Little could anybody guess that this was to be Villeneuve's final race outing in front of his home crowd. Eight months later he would be killed while practising in his Ferrari turbo at Zolder in preparation for the Belgian Grand Prix. The entire racing world mourned the passing of this brilliantly gifted young man, and the Montreal race organizers marked the tragic occasion by renaming their track the Circuit Gilles Villeneuve in time for the 1982 Canadian Grand Prix.

As if that season had not been scarred enough by tragedy, the Canadian Grand Prix was to be marked by another terrible accident. Villeneuve's former team-mate, Didier Pironi, stalled his pole-position Ferrari and, while the pack dodged in all directions to miss the stationary car, it was hit squarely by Ricardo Paletti's Osella. Having started from the back of the grid, Paletti had reached almost 100mph (160kmph) at the point of impact.

The race was immediately red-flagged to a halt while medical teams moved in to tend the grievously injured Italian driver. Paletti was eventually airlifted to hospital by helicopter, but succumbed to his injuries soon afterwards. The race was duly restarted in the gathering gloom towards evening and Nelson Piquet raced to a commanding victory behind the wheel of his Brabham-BMW turbo.

A varied cross-section of winners were thrown up by the Canadian race over the next few years. In 1983 it was René Arnoux's turn to triumph for Ferrari, followed by Piquet again for Brabham-BMW in 1984, while Michele Alboreto scored another Ferrari victory in 1985. In 1986 it was Nigel Mansell's turn, then the race missed a year in 1987 before the track was reshaped to accommodate the new pit complex in 1988, when Ayrton Senna emerged the winner in a McLaren-Honda.

While practising for the 1988 race, Derek Warwick crashed heavily in his Arrows-BMW at the fast S-bend adjacent to the new pit entrance. Subsequently, this section of the circuit was reshaped to slow the corner significantly. Despite these modifications, it was still one of the most tricky sections of the circuit, as Nigel Mansell was to discover to his cost while challenging Senna's McLaren for the lead of the 1992 race.

The English driver got off the racing line and on to the dust as he attempted to outbrake his Brazilian rival, lost control of his car and went bouncing across the gravel trap on the inside of the turn before spinning to a halt in front of the pits. Mansell was not amused by the incident, but Senna, who later retired from the race, shrugged aside any accusations that he had squeezed his rival and deprived him of racing room.

Further changes in the interests of safety were made to the Circuit Gilles Villeneuve for 1996, when the son of the man who gave his name to the track made his first F1 appearance in front of his home crowd in a Williams FW19. On this occasion he finished second behind his team-mate Damon Hill, but in 1977 he inexplicably spun off on the second lap while chasing the Ferrari of the eventual winner, Michael Schumacher.

EVERYTHING CLICKS TOGETHER'

Gilles Villeneuve's Ferrari 312T3 went on to win the 1978 Canadian Grand Prix. After the Canadian driver's death, the circuit was renamed in his memory.

FRANCE

CIRCUIT DE NEVERS, MAGNY-COURS

CIRCUIT LENGTH:
2.640 miles (4.250km).
LAP RECORD:
Nigel Mansell
(3.5 Williams–Renault FW14B), 1m 17.070s,
123.355mph (198.521kmph).
Lap record established in 1992.

CIRCUIT ASSESSMENT by MIKA HAKKINEN:

'This is a complex circuit, which offers plenty of chances to overtake if you are really decisive, but other sections are a little on the tight side. It is extremely well surfaced, and has excellent facilities, and some very demanding corners indeed.'

OF ALL THE RACES CONTAINED IN THIS VOLUME, THE FRENCH GRAND PRIX HAS PURSUED THE MOST NOMADIC EXISTENCE OF ALL DURING THE 46-SEASON HISTORY OF THE OFFICIAL F1 WORLD CHAMPIONSHIP. DURING THAT PERIOD, THE RACE HAS BEEN HELD AT REIMS-GUEUX, ROUEN-LES ESSARTS, CLERMONT-FERRAND, THE BUGATTI CIRCUIT AT LE MANS, DIJON-PRENOIS, PAUL RICARD AND, SINCE 1991, ON THE CIRCUIT DE NEVERS, NEAR MAGNY-COURS.

Regional political lobbying has often been the cause of this shifting from track to track, with influential figures in the various regional departments all competing to ensure that one of France's most prestigious sporting events is held in their neck of the woods. The Circuit de Nevers is geographically almost in the very centre of the country and has proved an enormous commercial success since Nigel Mansell emerged triumphant from the first French Grand Prix to be held there in 1991.

In 1992, Mansell repeated his victory *en route* to his F1 World Championship title, since when the race has been won by his Williams team successor Alain Prost, twice consecutively by Michael Schumacher's Benetton and, most recently, in 1995 by Damon Hill's Williams.

Damon Hill takes a turn ahead of his Williams team-mate, Alain Prost, as they swing into the Adelaide hairpin during the 1993 French Grand Prix. They finished the race taking first and second places.

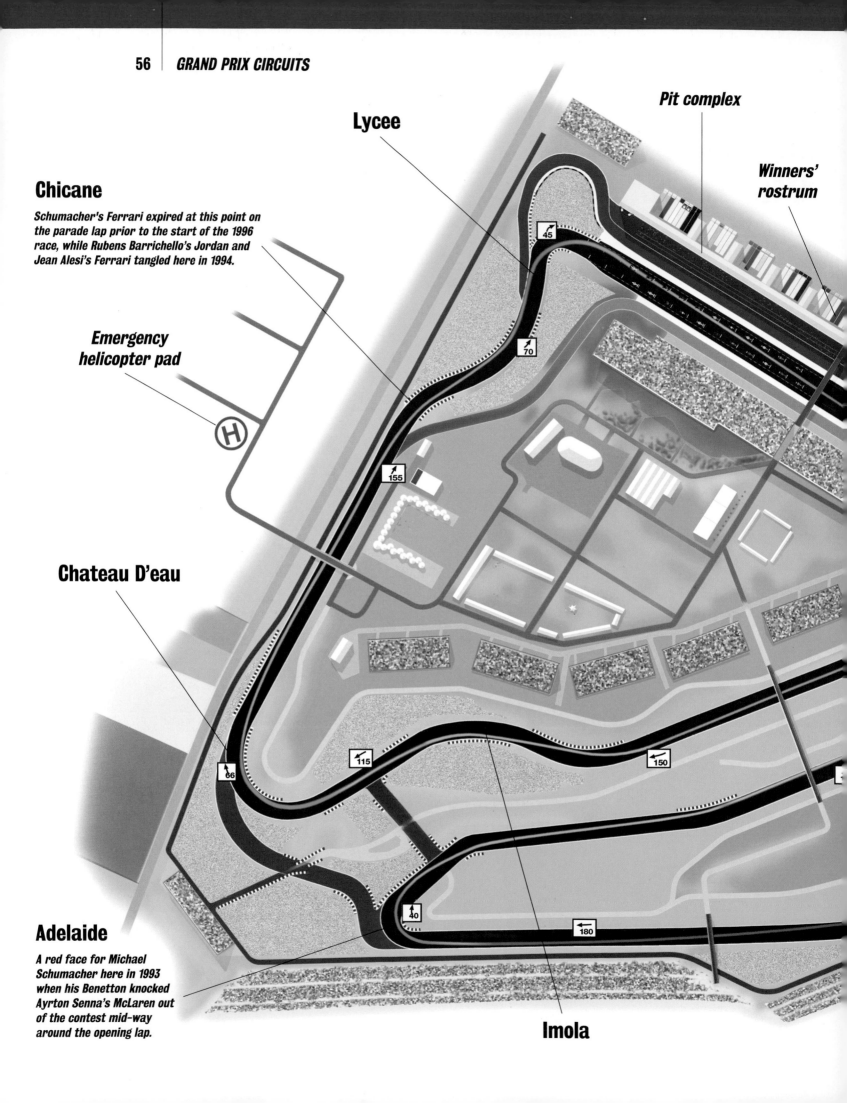

Lycee

Pit complex

Winners' rostrum

Chicane

Schumacher's Ferrari expired at this point on the parade lap prior to the start of the 1996 race, while Rubens Barrichello's Jordan and Jean Alesi's Ferrari tangled here in 1994.

Emergency helicopter pad

Chateau D'eau

Adelaide

A red face for Michael Schumacher here in 1993 when his Benetton knocked Ayrton Senna's McLaren out of the contest mid-way around the opening lap.

Imola

FRENCH GRAND PRIX CIRCUIT DE NEVERS, MAGNY-COURS

CIRCUIT LENGTH:
2.640 miles (4.250km)

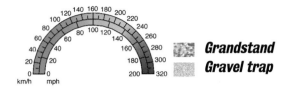

Grandstand
Gravel trap

= mph

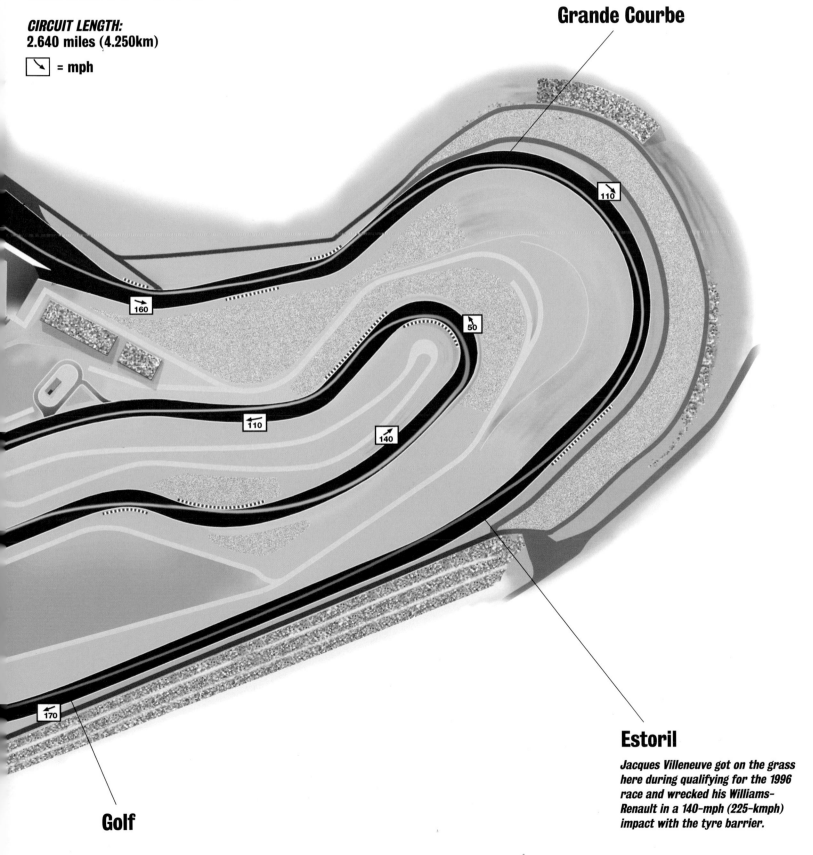

Grande Courbe

Estoril

Jacques Villeneuve got on the grass here during qualifying for the 1996 race and wrecked his Williams-Renault in a 140-mph (225-kmph) impact with the tyre barrier.

Golf

One of the great joys of starting from scratch with a totally new circuit design is the ability to produce a track surface as smooth as a billiard table. In that respect, the Magny-Cours' promoters have done an excellent job, which has attracted considerable praise from all the competing drivers. It has also particularly benefited the French Ligier F1 team, which has its headquarters adjacent to the circuit, making it particularly convenient for testing and development work.

The most unusual single feature of the Circuit de Nevers must surely be the ultra-tight sequence of S-bends that leads into the final right-hander before the start/finish line. Approached over a downhill brow, it frequently prompts bouts of over-ambitious driving on the part of competitors eager to make up places in the closing stages of the race. In that respect, the final gravel trap before the last corner – which is immediately in front of the pits – inevitably sees a lot of action.

Elsewhere, the circuit is wide and flowing, with generous run-off areas separating the tarmac from vertical concrete retaining walls. In many respects, this makes a long-distance view of the circuit look much like Dungeness beach and the cause of safety means that the spectators are generally positioned a long way from the cars. That is a shame, because it tends to devalue the challenging nature of several corners, most notably the high-speed, double-apex Grande Courbe and Estoril right-handers, which lead out on to the long, if gently curving, back straight.

It is through this section of the track that an ace driver can really make up time, slipstreaming up on to the tail of a rival before attempting to overtake under hard braking for the Adelaide hairpin. Even the most

First lap of the 1994 French Grand Prix with Michael Schumacher's Benetton turning into the Adelaide hairpin ahead of the Williams-Renaults of Damon Hill and Nigel Mansell.

gifted performers can make mistakes braking from high speed at this point, and in 1993 Schumacher emerged with an extremely red face after ramming Ayrton Senna's McLaren, sending both cars off the road at the start of a multiple accident. As a result, stern words of advice were later offered by Senna to his brilliant, if much less experienced, colleague.

On the fast exit of Estoril, the 1995 race also saw an unfortunate moment when Damon Hill – leading in the opening stages – had to back off suddenly as he came up to lap the much slower Forti Corse of Luca Badoer. Unfortunately, at that precise moment, Schumacher's Benetton was inches behind Hill's Williams, and when the Englishman suddenly slowed up, Michael wrongly concluded that his rival was playing dirty by giving him a 'brake test'.

Thankfully, the two men later resolved their differences. In 1997 Hill won commandingly for Williams, while Schumacher, now in a Ferrari, broke down on the parade lap. A year on, Schumacher won convincingly, with Hill nowhere in sight.

The start of the inaugural 1991 French Grand Prix at Magny-Cours, with Alain Prost's Ferrari sweeping into the first left-hander of the circuit.

BRITAIN

SILVERSTONE CIRCUIT, NEAR TOWCESTER

FORMER CIRCUIT LENGTH: 3.152 miles (5.072km).
LAP RECORD: Jacques Villeneuve (3.0 Williams–Renault FW18),
1m 29.288s, 127.068mph (204.497kmph).
Lap record established in 1996.
CURRENT CIRCUIT LENGTH: 3.194 miles (5.140km).
LAP RECORD: Michael Schumacher (3.0 Ferrari F310B),
1m 24.475s, 136.109mph (219.047kmph).
Lap record established in 1997.

CIRCUIT ASSESSMENT by JOHNNY HERBERT:
'Understandably, this is a great favourite for me. Immensely challenging with some really daunting high-speed corners, but recent safety modifications have certainly made it extremely difficult to overtake. A real driver's circuit.'

IN THE AFTERMATH OF THE SECOND WORLD WAR, BRITAIN WAS SORELY LACKING WHEN IT CAME TO VENUES FOR MOTOR RACING. THE OLD BANKED CIRCUIT AT BROOKLANDS LAY ABANDONED AND DONINGTON PARK, WHICH WAS THE VENUE FOR THE EPIC MERCEDES VERSUS AUTO UNION BATTLES IN THE LATE 1930S, HAD BEEN TURNED INTO A MILITARY VEHICLE DUMP AND WOULD NOT BE RESUSCITATED FOR RACING PURPOSES FOR A FURTHER 30 YEARS.

It was, therefore, no surprise that the motor-sport fraternity turned its hand to the task of adapting redundant RAF airfields for racing. The most famous by far would be Silverstone, near Towcester, the perimeter roads and abandoned runways of which were first used in 1947 to produce a twisting 3.7-mile (5.95-km) lap. Silverstone was used for the first post-war British Grand Prix that same year. By 1949, the layout had been altered to include only the perimeter roads, a configuration that has been effectively developed to this day.

In 1952 Silverstone's length was adjusted to 2.93 miles (4.72km) when the pits were moved to beyond the Woodcote corner, the high-speed right-hand turn that still leads drivers into their lap of the circuit. Unfortunately, in 1963 a race official standing in

Gerhard Berger's Ferrari sweeps through Luffield corner during the 1994 British Grand Prix at Silverstone. This tight infield section of the track has been progressively upgraded for added safety and better racing in the years since Ayrton Senna's death.

BRITISH GRAND PRIX SILVERSTONE CIRCUIT, NEAR TOWCESTER

CIRCUIT LENGTH:
3.194 miles (5.140km)

= mph

Abbey Curve

The Vale

140 160 180
120 200
100 220
80 240
60 260
40 40 280
20 20 300
0 0 320
km/h mph

Grandstand
Gravel trap

85

175

160

Club

Club corner is a particularly challenging point on the circuit since the cars are under hard acceleration while exiting this fast right-hander, which has a rather narrow run-off area on the outside. This is a point on the circuit where crucial tenths of a second can be made or lost.

105

180

Stowe

Hanger Straight

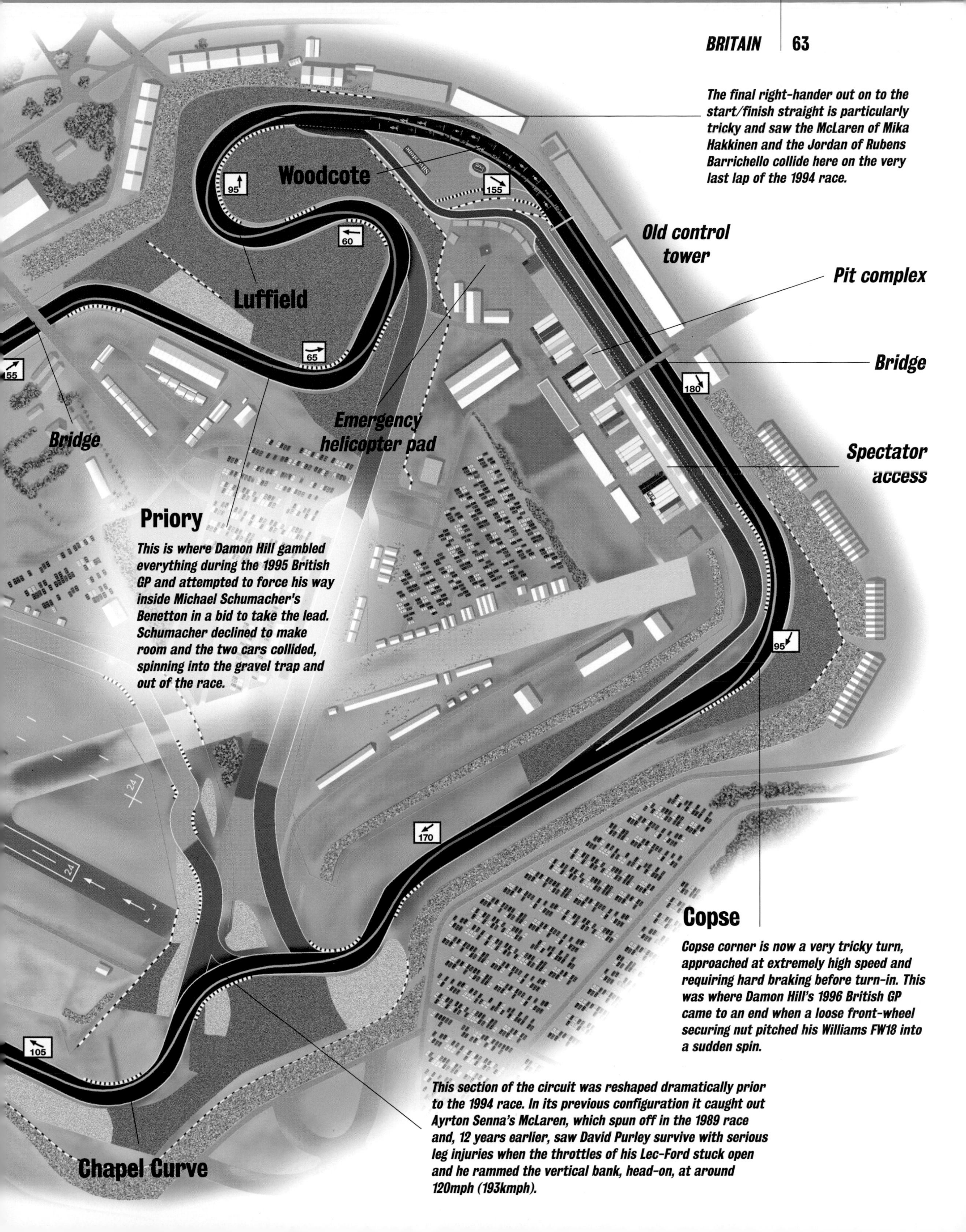

The final right-hander out on to the start/finish straight is particularly tricky and saw the McLaren of Mika Hakkinen and the Jordan of Rubens Barrichello collide here on the very last lap of the 1994 race.

95

Woodcote

155

60

Luffield

Old control tower

65

Pit complex

Bridge

155

Bridge

Emergency helicopter pad

180

Spectator access

95

Priory

This is where Damon Hill gambled everything during the 1995 British GP and attempted to force his way inside Michael Schumacher's Benetton in a bid to take the lead. Schumacher declined to make room and the two cars collided, spinning into the gravel trap and out of the race.

170

Copse

Copse corner is now a very tricky turn, approached at extremely high speed and requiring hard braking before turn-in. This was where Damon Hill's 1996 British GP came to an end when a loose front-wheel securing nut pitched his Williams FW18 into a sudden spin.

105

This section of the circuit was reshaped dramatically prior to the 1994 race. In its previous configuration it caught out Ayrton Senna's McLaren, which spun off in the 1989 race and, 12 years earlier, saw David Purley survive with serious leg injuries when the throttles of his Lec-Ford stuck open and he rammed the vertical bank, head-on, at around 120mph (193kmph).

Chapel Curve

The start of the 1994 British Grand Prix with eventual winner Damon Hill's Williams accelerating away from pole position ahead of Michael Schumacher's Benetton. The long, sweeping nature of Woodcote corner can be seen stretching away behind the pack.

'IMMENSELY CHALLENGING, WITH SOME DAUNTING

Nigel Mansell's Ferrari 640 heads for second place in the 1989 British Grand Prix at Silverstone. The Englishman had to give way to Alain Prost's McLaren on this occasion.

front of the pit counter was killed when a competing car lost control on the exit of Woodcote and spun into him.

This sad incident prompted the construction of a completely new, elevated pit lane in time for the 1964 season, but Woodcote remained a dauntingly quick corner, which, although enormously challenging to the competitors, looked as though it was asking for trouble should a driver lose control of his mount while running in close company with other cars.

These fears were eventually realized in 1973 when the South African Jody Scheckter lost control of his McLaren M23 at the end of the opening lap of the British Grand Prix. Sliding wide on to the grass as he came out of Woodcote, Scheckter's car was pitched into a spin and speared back across the track to collide with the pit wall.

The closely bunched pack scattered in all directions, triggering a multiple collision that brought the race to a halt. It took the best part of an hour for the Brabham driver Andrea de Adamich to be cut from his car with two broken legs. But he survived to make a full recovery, and most observers believed that the outcome could have been a whole lot worse.

Ever since 1964, when Brands Hatch hosted the British Grand Prix, the country's most important international motor race had been shared with the Kent circuit on an alternate-year basis. By the time the Grand Prix returned in 1975 a chicane had been installed in Woodcote and all the pit buildings had been demolished and replaced by a state-of-the-art complex fronting a much wider pit lane.

Close finishes had been established as something of a Silverstone tradition, but the 1975 British Grand

HIGH-SPEED CORNERS. A REAL DRIVER'S CIRCUIT'

Michael Schumacher swoops into Stowe corner ahead of Damon Hill and Gerhard Berger in the opening stages of the 1994 British Grand Prix.

Prix ended in chaos when a thunderstorm doused the circuit and most of the field slithered into the catch fencing at Club corner. Brazil's Emerson Fittipaldi managed to keep control to win at the wheel of his McLaren, and two years later it was James Hunt's turn to win the Silverstone race during the course of his World Championship year.

The next major change to the circuit came in time for the 1989 Grand Prix race when a tight chicane was installed before Woodcote corner and, in 1992, the section between Stowe and Club corners was extensively modified in order to provide a more interesting section of track in front of the newly installed spectators' viewing banks.

These changes attracted mixed feelings from both spectators and drivers, although the latter were somehow in two minds on the subject. On the one hand, the drivers relished the flat-out blast down to Stowe, and the following straight down to Club, where overtaking could at least be considered. On the other hand, they continued to be mindful of the high speeds involved at the British circuit, a factor that was thrown into sharp relief after Pedro Lamy crashed his Lotus during testing in early 1994 and ended up vaulting a retaining fence and landing in a spectator tunnel. This potential disaster provided added impetus to the programme of safety improvements in the run-up to that year's British Grand Prix.

The infield loop immediately before Woodcote was also regarded as a mixed blessing. To watch F1 cars stuttering along in second and third gears, along a short straight between medium-speed corners, was hardly stimulating for those who recalled Silverstone in its high-speed heyday. The racing was definitely not so good.

In 1995, these changes were followed by the reprofiling of both Stowe and Copse corners, but the overall effect was to make overtaking difficult in the extreme. This problem was addressed in time for the 1997 race, and further modifications were made to improve overtaking. A close-fought race ensued, with Jacques Villeneuve emerging victorious to score the Williams team's 100th GP victory, on the 18th anniversary of the team's first victory on the track.

The grid lines up for the start of the 1996 British Grand Prix, with the Williams FW18s of Damon Hill and Jacques Villeneuve together on the front row.

In the aftermath of Senna's death, Silverstone responded with admirable efficiency to the FIA's requests that circuit safety be improved at every track on the calendar, the British venue making enormous changes at short notice in time for the 1994 race. These involved a slower infield loop section before Woodcote and revisions to the fast Becketts section.

GERMANY

HOCKENHEIMRING, NEAR HEIDELBERG

CIRCUIT LENGTH:
4.239 miles (6.823km).
LAP RECORD:
Gerhard Berger
(3.0 Benetton Renault B197), 1m 45.747s,
144.33mph (232.27kmph).
Lap record established in 1997.

CIRCUIT ASSESSMENT by MICHAEL SCHUMACHER:
'On the face of it, Hockenheim looks remarkably straightforward, but it is really quite difficult to work out the perfect balance between straight-line speed and aerodynamic downforce when you are setting up the chassis. The chicanes are very fast indeed and it is important to try keeping away from the kerbs as much as possible.'

H OCKENHEIM EMERGED AS THE PERMANENT HOME OF THE GERMAN GRAND PRIX IN 1977, A YEAR AFTER NIKI LAUDA'S FERRARI HAD CRASHED IN FLAMES ON THE OLD NÜRBURGRING, CRUELLY EXPOSING THE PROBLEMS OF EFFECTIVELY MARSHALLING THE DRAMATIC 14-MILE (22.5-KM) CIRCUIT THAT WENDS ITS WAY THROUGH THE SPECTACULAR EIFEL MOUNTAINS.

It was, therefore, ironic that, just 12 months after cheating death, it was Lauda who won the 1977 race at Hockenheim, back behind the wheel of a Ferrari. Yet, while the Nürburgring had come to be regarded as the ultimate challenge to both car and driver, Hockenheim was already damned in the minds of most drivers as the circuit that claimed the life of the legendary Jimmy Clark, killed in a minor-league Formula 2 race there in April 1968.

Hockenheim was originally used as long ago as 1939. At that time the circuit was simply two long straights through the intimidating pine forests, linked by a hairpin (actually in Hockenheim village) at the lower end, and a fast right-hander – known as the Ostkurve – at the opposite end of the track.

Johnny Herbert's Sauber leads Olivier Panis in the Ligier and Mika Salo's Tyrrell through the tight Sachskurve hairpin during the 1996 German Grand Prix. The huge, permanent grandstand was filled to capacity.

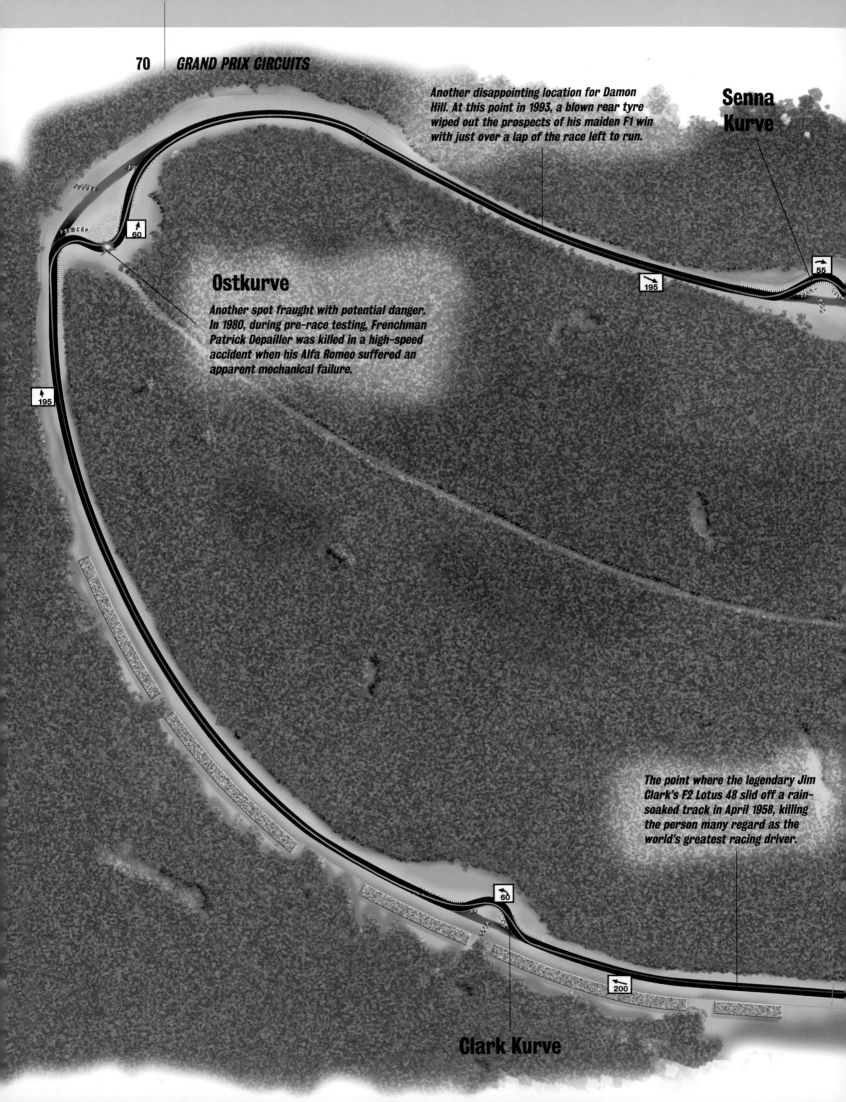

Another disappointing location for Damon Hill. At this point in 1993, a blown rear tyre wiped out the prospects of his maiden F1 win with just over a lap of the race left to run.

Senna Kurve

Ostkurve

Another spot fraught with potential danger. In 1980, during pre-race testing, Frenchman Patrick Depailler was killed in a high-speed accident when his Alfa Romeo suffered an apparent mechanical failure.

60

195

195

55

The point where the legendary Jim Clark's F2 Lotus 48 slid off a rain-soaked track in April 1958, killing the person many regard as the world's greatest racing driver.

60

200

Clark Kurve

GERMAN GRAND PRIX
HOCKENHEIMRING, NEAR HEIDELBERG

CIRCUIT LENGTH:
4.239 miles (6.823km)

↘ = mph

Mark Blundell had a nasty 190-mph (306-kmph) moment here in 1993 when his Ligier was edged on to the grass by Gerhard Berger's Ferrari as the two men battled for a top six placing. Sharp words were exchanged after the race!

Agip Kurve

Opel Kurve

Sachskurve

Pit complex

Emergency helicopter pad

Nordkurve

Another bad corner for Damon Hill, where his Williams spun off the road while leading into the second lap of the 1995 German GP. A year earlier, almost half the field was eliminated in a multiple collision at this same point.

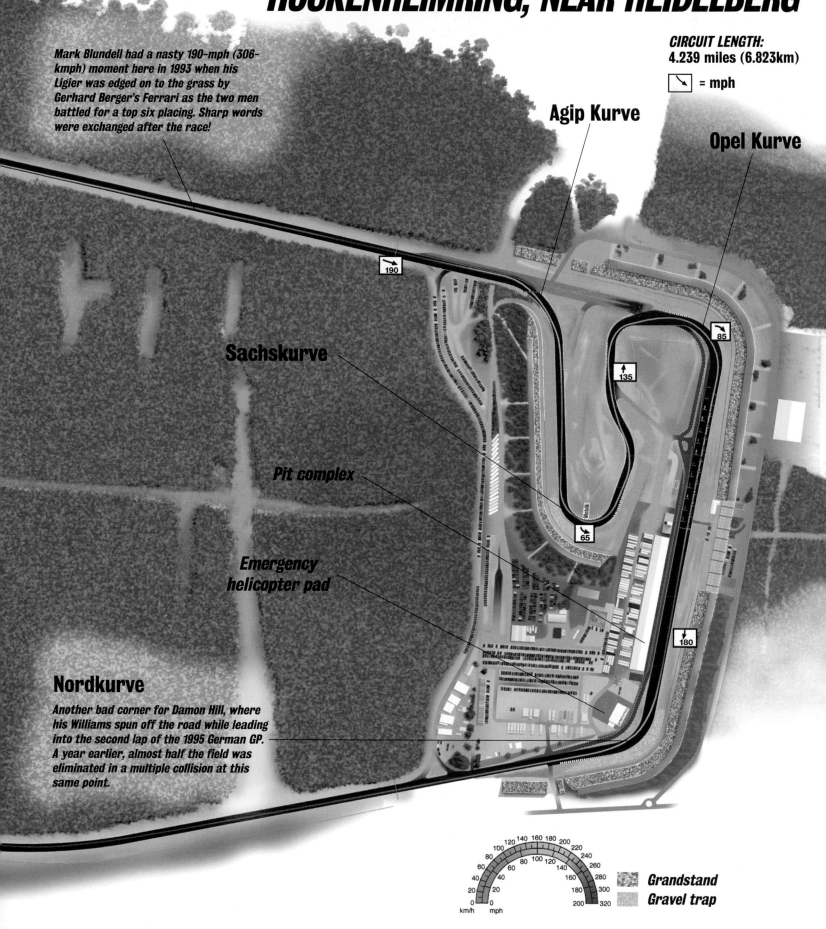

Grandstand
Gravel trap

Nigel Mansell's Williams is dwarfed by the Hockenheim pine trees during the 1992 German Grand Prix.

However, at about this time the local government purchased the lower half of the Hockenheim track in order to facilitate the construction of a new *autobahn*. Their fortunes boosted by the lavish compensation involved in the deal, the Hockenheim authorities developed a shortened version of their track, now incorporating a tight infield section flanked by massive permanent concrete grandstands capable of accommodating more than 80,000 spectators.

With the unfailing benefit of hindsight, the circuit was spectacularly unsafe for the drivers. Long straights out through the pine forests offered no protection whatsoever in terms of catch fencing or guard rails. There was just a narrow ribbon of tarmac, a few feet of grass either side, and then the unyielding, tightly packed trees.

Circuit safety was only just becoming a major issue in the late 1960s, but the march of progress was too late to save Jim Clark. On Sunday, 7 April 1968, the day dawned dank and overcast, with a curtain of rain hanging over Hockenheim to produce an overwhelming air of gloom and foreboding.

Jim Clark had originally intended to race a Ford F3L

Mercedes-Benz used it to test their new 1.5-litre cars, which would be used solely and specifically for that year's Tripoli Grand Prix.

After the Second World War, national-level racing resumed at the track near Heidelberg, but its bland nature could match neither the Nürburgring nor the spectacular Solitude road circuit near Stuttgart, which also hosted Formula 1 non-Championship races through to the mid-1960s.

prototype sports car at Brands Hatch that day, but a late change of plan brought him to Germany to compete at the wheel of a works F2 Lotus 48. In the first of the two heats, the 32-year-old Scot left the road on the outward leg of the circuit and crashed into the trees at 130mph (210kmph). He didn't stand a chance.

Hockenheim stood condemned from that day onwards. Clark's death was front-page news throughout the world. His rivals trembled. Jimmy had been regarded as inviolate. If he could be killed behind the wheel, then what chance was there for the rest of them?

Two years later, while safety improvements were made at the Nürburgring, Hockenheim hosted the German Grand Prix for the first time. Ironically, it proved to be a brilliant, two-car battle between Jacky Ickx's Ferrari and one of the superb Lotus 72s driven by the German-born Austrian Jochen Rindt. Delighting the capacity crowd, Rindt won by a couple of lengths on the final lap.

In the aftermath of this race, Hockenheim was further altered with chicanes positioned on the two long straights through the forests. The Grand Prix duly returned in 1977, after which there was a further tragedy during testing immediately prior to the start of the 1980 race.

Frenchman Patrick Depailler suffered a major mechanical failure at 150mph (240kmph) approaching the Ostkurve in his F1 Alfa Romeo. The hapless driver was killed in the ensuing impact with the guard rail, a disaster that inevitably ensured that the subsequent German Grand Prix was conducted in an understandably subdued atmosphere.

Depailler's death resulted in another chicane being installed at the Ostkurve, yet Hockenheim's main problem – the sheer speed attained by Grand Prix cars on the straights – continued to haunt every competitor. This factor was a major issue in the wet, when clouds of spray hung in the air along these high-speed corridors between the trees, as Didier Pironi discovered to his cost when his Ferrari plunged into the back of Alain Prost's Renault during a rain-soaked practice session for the 1982 Grand Prix.

The impact sent the scarlet Italian machine rocketing skywards, before plunging back to the tarmac on its nose. It took a long time before Pironi was delicately cut from the wreckage. Pironi lived, but his racing days were over and he underwent more than 30 operations on his legs before he could walk again.

Yet Hockenheim survives and prospers to this day. The track benefits from being close to several large German cities and always attracts enormous crowds as a result – none more so than the 130,000 fans who regularly camp out and make a weekend of it for the Grand Prix each summer.

With Michael Schumacher to cheer as their hero, the Germans at last have their very own, home-grown World Champion. In 1997, Schumacher finished second to extend his World Championship points lead, but Austrian veteran Gerhard Berger scored a runaway victory from pole position in a Benetton, a successful return after a three-race break caused by a sinus infection.

The crowds are ecstatic and on their feet – so it must be Schumacher. German fans at last have their own double World Champion to cheer on their home soil.

HUNGARY

HUNGARORING, NEAR BUDAPEST

CIRCUIT LENGTH:
2.466 miles (3.968km).
LAP RECORD:
Nigel Mansell
(3.5 Williams–Renault FW14B), 1m 18.308s,
113.349mph (182.418kmph).
Lap record established in 1992.

CIRCUIT ASSESSMENT by JEAN ALESI:

'To record a quick lap, or capitalize on any overtaking opportunity, this is a circuit that demands patience and precision. The only real chance to pass presents itself at the end of the start/finish straight and that relies on a perfect exit from the uphill right-hander that leads on to that section. You have to judge things to perfection, or you can be left trailing around in a traffic jam.'

HUNGARY WAS THE FIRST OF THE EASTERN BLOC NATIONS TO GRACE ITS SPORTING CALENDAR WITH A ROUND OF THE OFFICIAL FORMULA 1 WORLD CHAMPIONSHIP IN 1986, WHEN THE FIRST GRAND PRIX WAS STAGED AT THE TWISTY LITTLE HUNGARORING CIRCUIT, ABOUT 12 MILES (19.3KM) FROM THE CENTRE OF BUDAPEST.

The first serious motor-sporting events in Hungary had been held during the 1950s in the form of hill-climbs and, by the mid-1960s, a street circuit was laid out in Budapest to host rounds of the then prestigious European Touring Car Championship. However, it was not until 1983 that F1 Constructors' Association President, Bernie Ecclestone, began talks with the Hungarian government about the possibility of building a permanent circuit that conformed to current international standards.

By the start of 1985, the Hungaroring was completed and in September of that year an agreement was concluded to stage a round of the World Championship for five consecutive years, starting in

The best view at Hungaroring is across the tight hairpin behind the paddock. Here, Keke Rosberg's McLaren leads Stefan Johansson's Ferrari, Riccardo Patrese's Brabham and Michele Alboreto's Ferrari early on during the 1986 Hungarian Grand Prix, the first such event to be staged.

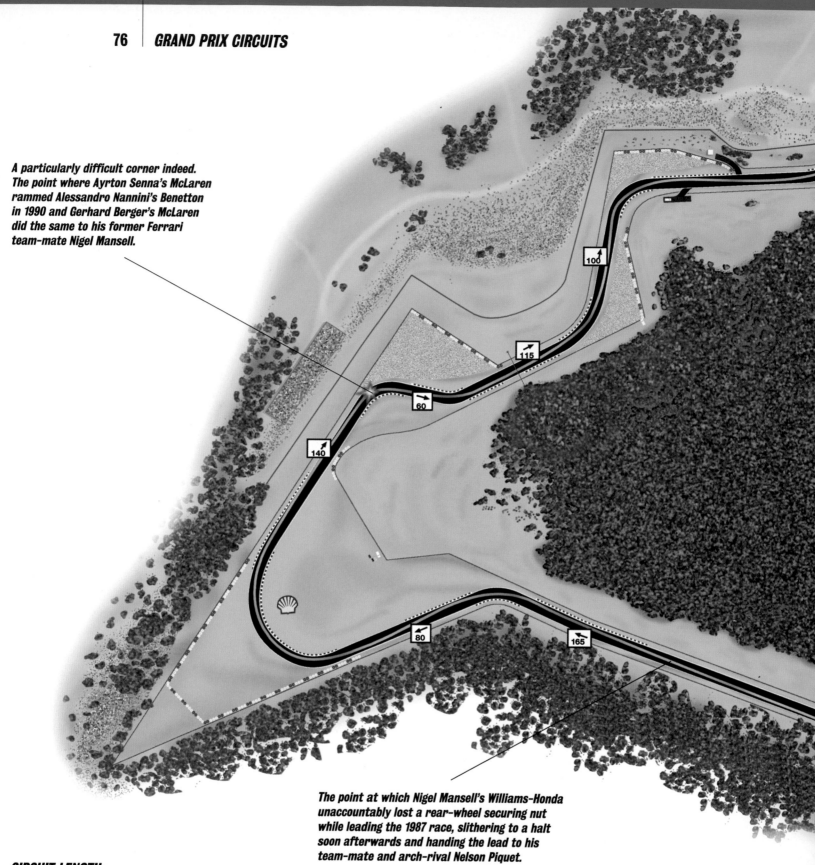

A particularly difficult corner indeed. The point where Ayrton Senna's McLaren rammed Alessandro Nannini's Benetton in 1990 and Gerhard Berger's McLaren did the same to his former Ferrari team-mate Nigel Mansell.

The point at which Nigel Mansell's Williams-Honda unaccountably lost a rear-wheel securing nut while leading the 1987 race, slithering to a halt soon afterwards and handing the lead to his team-mate and arch-rival Nelson Piquet.

CIRCUIT LENGTH:
2.466 miles (3.968km)

 = mph

HUNGARIAN GRAND PRIX
HUNGARORING, NEAR BUDAPEST

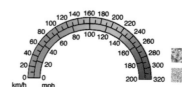

 Grandstand
Gravel trap

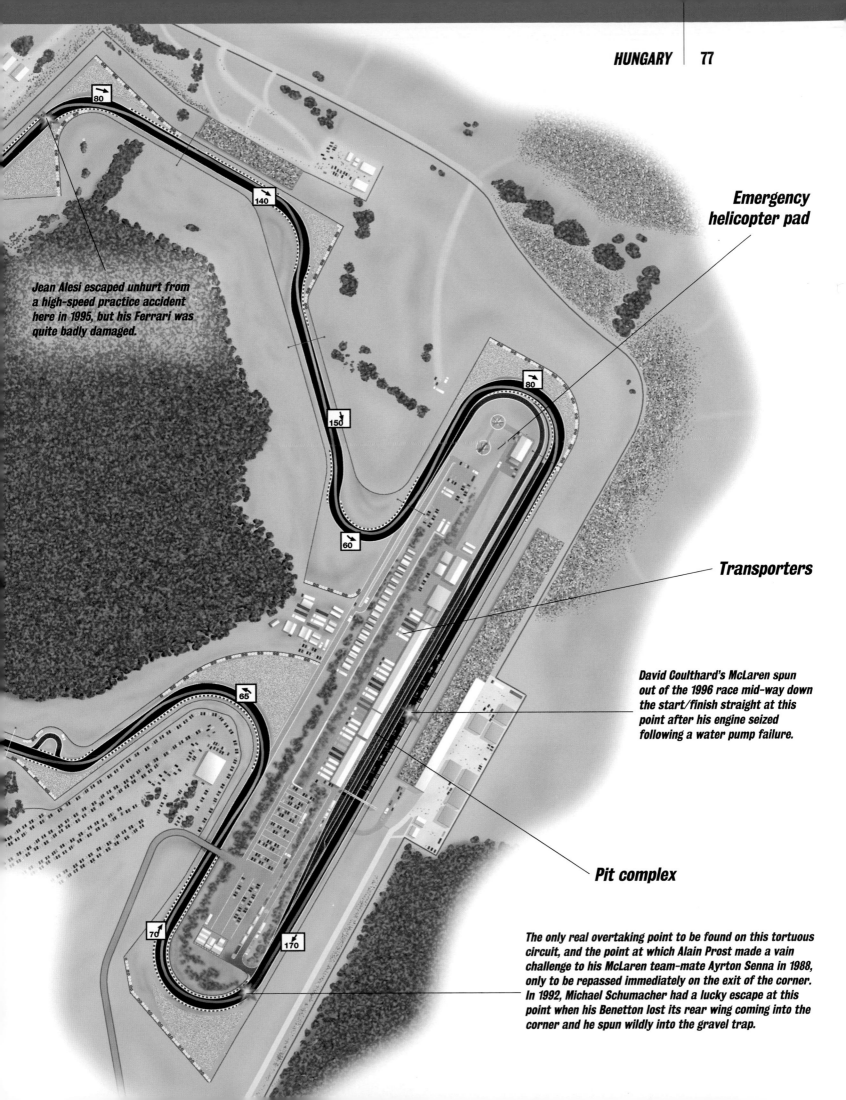

Emergency helicopter pad

Jean Alesi escaped unhurt from a high-speed practice accident here in 1995, but his Ferrari was quite badly damaged.

Transporters

David Coulthard's McLaren spun out of the 1996 race mid-way down the start/finish straight at this point after his engine seized following a water pump failure.

Pit complex

The only real overtaking point to be found on this tortuous circuit, and the point at which Alain Prost made a vain challenge to his McLaren team-mate Ayrton Senna in 1988, only to be repassed immediately on the exit of the corner. In 1992, Michael Schumacher had a lucky escape at this point when his Benetton lost its rear wing coming into the corner and he spun wildly into the gravel trap.

1986. Among the drivers and competing teams, the initial response to the Hungaroring was mixed. The general consensus was that it was far too tight and difficult to overtake, while a build-up of thick dust off the racing line made it extremely hard for competitors to dive inside their rivals into the various tight corners.

The first race produced a victory for Nelson Piquet's Williams-Honda, but not before Ayrton Senna's Lotus-Renault had led the race for many laps. Piquet eventually slipped past and took the lead while going into the tricky downhill, 180-degree right-hander at the end of the start/finish straight – a position on the Hungaroring that would eventually be established as probably the only point where overtaking was consistently possible.

In 1987, Piquet repeated that initial success, only winning after his Williams team-mate Nigel Mansell retired from the lead when a rear wheel worked loose after the car lost one of the retaining bolts from its rear hub. In 1988, the crowds were treated to a fantastic duel between the McLaren-Hondas of Ayrton Senna and Alain Prost, the Brazilian winning after the Frenchman successfully executed a bold overtaking move going into that first corner. He took the lead only to run wide on the exit and have his team-mate pass him. From then on, Senna kept the inside

line into that corner well guarded, and Prost was never presented with another opportunity to have a second bite at the cherry.

Undoubtedly the most electrifying Hungarian Grand Prix took place in 1989, by which time Nigel Mansell had switched from Williams to Ferrari. During the first qualifying session on Friday, Mansell concluded that he had made incorrect adjustments to the chassis set-up of his Ferrari 640, which had prevented him bidding for a competitive grid position.

Mindful of the problems involved in overtaking at Hungaroring, he effectively abandoned his efforts to challenge for pole position in Saturday's second qualifying session. Instead, he spent his time concentrating on the very best set-up he could work out for the race. He qualified 12th, starting the race on the sixth row of the grid, but correctly judged that he would be in a good position to make the most of whatever overtaking opportunities presented themselves.

As Riccardo Patrese's Williams accelerated ahead of Ayrton Senna's McLaren at the start, so Mansell was already making up ground. His Ferrari completed the opening lap in eighth place, then moved ahead of Alessandro Nannini's Benetton to take seventh on the 11th lap. By lap 30 he was up to third place, and then, when Patrese retired, he moved into second place behind Senna on lap 53 of the 77-lap race.

On lap 58 of the race, Senna found himself momentarily wrong-footed as he came up to lap Stefan Johansson's much slower Onyx-Ford. He backed off on the throttle for a split second and Mansell, by then right on the tail of his McLaren, surged through the gap that momentarily opened up ahead of him. Thereafter, the Ferrari roared away to an unchallenged victory as Senna, worried about his McLaren-Honda's high fuel consumption, had to ease off and settle for second place.

Senna would yet again play a pivotal role in the 1990 Hungarian Grand Prix, once more having to be satisfied with second-best after a performance that many Formula 1 insiders concluded emphasized the sheer absurdity of Hungaroring's layout. Having got away unscathed in a collision with Alessandro Nannini's Benetton, Senna went hell-for-leather after Thierry Boutsen's leading Williams, which was by then well in front of the following pack of drivers.

On a clear track, Senna was able to circulate almost two seconds a lap faster than Boutsen, but when he caught the Williams there was simply no way to pass him. The Belgian was handling his car with tremendous precision and refused to be ruffled by Senna's ominous presence in his mirrors. As long as Boutsen kept his cool, there was just no chance for Senna to make a bid for the lead. So it proved to be, with the Williams driver coming in a worthy winner and Senna a fuming, frustrated second.

In 1991 and 1992 Senna won for McLaren again, the latter event marking Nigel Mansell's accession to the World Championship title. In 1993 it was Damon Hill's turn to score his very first Grand Prix victory at Budapest, an unchallenged run from start to finish after his then Williams team-mate, Alain Prost, stalled on the grid prior to the final parade lap and had to start from the back of the pack.

Michael Schumacher's terrific precision in the Benetton-Ford B194 yielded a dominant victory over Hill in 1994, but Hill turned the tables in 1995, only for the Englishman to be beaten again in a close sprint for the winning line in 1996 by his new Williams team-mate Jacques Villeneuve.

All these races again served to emphasize the acute difficulty involved in executing any sort of overtaking manoeuvre at the Hungaroring, so on this particular circuit, pit-stop strategy is even more important than ever. In the closing stages of the 1996 race, Hill was allowed to get within striking distance of Villeneuve's winning Williams when the Canadian driver was delayed by a sticking wheel nut at his final refuelling stop. As it transpired, he eventually got out ahead of his team-mate, but there would have been little chance of regaining his lead had he been delayed by only a few more seconds.

The pit-lane exit opens out into the braking area for that crucial first corner, so a clean getaway from a refuelling stop can make all the difference between retaining or losing a place. In this respect, the frustration of competing at Hungaroring is probably only matched by that experienced at Monaco.

Due to the confined topography of the circuit, the pits and paddock areas are positioned on different levels behind the pit-lane garages, and an enormous amount of complex manoeuvring is required to position the transporters for unloading purposes.

Victories at Hungaroring have often been achieved by the driver who can get ahead and then slow the pace of the opposition behind. However, the 1997 race provided a reversal of the established form. Damon Hill dominated the race in an Arrows-Yamaha, only losing to Villeneuve's Williams on the last lap when his car's hydraulic system went haywire, affecting both throttle and gearchange control. Hill eventually finished second after a brilliantly opportunistic performance on a day when the Goodyear tyres used by most of his key opposition blistered unexpectedly and lost grip in the searing heat.

Follow my leader. Roberto Moreno's Benetton, Gianni Morbidelli's Minardi, Ayrton Senna's McLaren and Pierluigi Martini's Minardi running nose-to-tail at the Hungaroring during the 1993 Grand Prix.

BELGIUM

CIRCUIT NATIONAL DE SPA-FRANCORCHAMPS

CIRCUIT LENGTH:
4.329 miles (6.968km).
LAP RECORD:
Alain Prost
(3.5 Williams-Renault FW15C), 1m 51.095s,
140.424mph (225.990kmph).
Lap record established in 1993.

CIRCUIT ASSESSMENT by MARTIN BRUNDLE:

'Absolutely one of my favourite circuits with some high-speed corners that really take your breath away, both metaphorically and physically. Spa is a real challenge and reminds you what being a Grand Prix driver is all about. It must rank as one of the most exhilarating places on earth at which to drive a Formula 1 car.'

THE SPA-FRANCORCHAMPS CIRCUIT, EVEN IN ITS CURRENT, TRUNCATED 4.329-MILE (6.968-KM) CONFIGURATION INTRODUCED IN 1983, REMAINS BY POPULAR ACCLAIM ONE OF THE VERY BEST VENUES ON THE FORMULA 1 WORLD CHAMPIONSHIP TRAIL. IT IS ALSO ONE OF THE OLDEST CIRCUITS CURRENTLY IN USE, HAVING FIRST HOSTED A MOTORCYCLE GRAND PRIX AS LONG AGO AS 1921 AND ITS FIRST RACE FOR GRAND PRIX CARS IN 1925.

Although sports- and touring-car races continued throughout the 1920s, it was not until 1933 that Grand Prix machinery made its reappearance on this dramatic track, with its 9-mile (14.5-km) lap along country roads around the Hautes-Fagnes region of southern Belgium. In 1939 it gained notoriety as the circuit that claimed the life of the brilliant British driver Dick Seaman, who crashed his Mercedes-Benz on the fast right-hand corner before the La Source hairpin and subsequently died from burns sustained when the car burst into flames.

The race was resurrected after the war on a slightly modified 8.9-mile (14.3-km) circuit and

Gerhard Berger's Benetton leads Mika Hakkinen's McLaren, Jean Alesi's Benetton and Martin Brundle's Jordan up the long 190-mph (306-kmph) blast from Eau Rouge to Les Combes during the opening laps of the 1996 Belgian Grand Prix.

Eau Rouge

Regarded as the most challenging corner on any circuit in the world. In 1993, Alessandro Zanardi had a huge 130-mph (209-kmph) shunt in his Lotus during practice, surviving with a broken tooth, and the corner was extensively modified thereafter to incorporate a much wider run-off area.

Pit complex

La Source

A really tricky corner, positioned as it is only a hundred yards or so away from the front row of the starting grid. In 1996, both the Sauber-Fords of Johnny Herbert and Heinz-Harald Frentzen were eliminated in a collision at this point.

Emergency helicopter pad

'Bus Stop'

The best overtaking opportunity on the circuit, under hard braking from around 180mph (290kmph) for the "Bus Stop" chicane. High kerbs at this point almost always contribute to undamaging spins.

CIRCUIT LENGTH:
4.329 miles (6.968km)

 = mph

BELGIAN GRAND PRIX CIRCUIT NATIONAL DE SPA-FRANCORCHAMPS

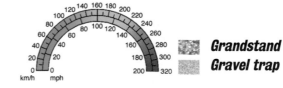

Grandstand
Gravel trap

→ 185

Les Combes

This was the point where Damon Hill and Michael Schumacher banged wheels during their battle for the lead of the 1995 Belgian GP. Hill later directed some well-aimed criticism of his German rival's tactics following the race.

Malmedy

→ 110

← 95

← 170

Michael Schumacher's Benetton spun here while leading the 1994 Belgian GP – although he continued, he was later disqualified from the race for a technical infringement.

Schumacher's Ferrari crashed here heavily during practice for the 1996 Belgian GP. It was a major impact, but the car spun in backwards and Schumacher escaped with only a shaking – and went on to win the race.

← 68

Rivage

→ 175

Fagnes

↗ 180

Blanchimont

Another scene of a Gerhard Berger/Mark Blundell collision in the 1993 Belgian GP.

↘ 105

← 135

Stavelot

'ONE OF THE MOST EXHILARATING PLACES

always proved a test of durability for driver and car alike. Between 1962 and 1965, the great Jim Clark's Lotus won four successive Belgian Grand Prix victories in widely varying weather conditions, a record subsequently matched by Ayrton Senna between 1988 and 1991 at the wheel of a McLaren-Honda.

Concern about heavy rain on this high-speed circuit was an abiding worry in the minds of most Grand Prix drivers and, in 1966, disaster struck when the cars accelerated away from the grid in dry conditions only to run into a cloudburst midway around the opening lap as they went on to the high-speed Masta straight.

Most of the field was eliminated in a succession of minor accidents, but Jackie Stewart's BRM crashed into an outside basement adjacent to a woodcutter's cottage on the edge of the Masta straight. The Scottish driver sustained several broken bones and was trapped in the wrecked car, soaked in leaking fuel, until he was rescued by fellow competitors Graham Hill and Bob Bondurant.

This episode was a seminal moment in post-war Grand Prix history. Stewart was the most promising rising star of his generation and his experience at Spa sparked a career-long commitment to enhancing

Shadow and light predominate as a McLaren speeds through the Belgian countryside on the downhill plunge towards Blanchimont.

safety standards in F1, the long-term legacy of which is still being felt in the final decade of the century.

Yet Stewart was by no means a softy. If he had any reservations about Spa's safety, he put them to one side and returned to finish the 1967 Belgian Grand Prix in second place behind Dan Gurney's Eagle, driving his unwieldy BRM H-16 one-handed for much of the race since he was having to hold his troublesome mount in gear almost from the start.

After Pedro Rodriguez scored a brilliant victory for the BRM team in 1970, Spa-Francorchamps was dropped from the Grand Prix trail. The much shorter tracks at Nivelles, near Brussels, and Zolder, near Hasselt, hosted the Belgian race between them in the years up until 1983, when the F1 fraternity returned to Spa to race on a shorter circuit that somehow managed to retain much of the charisma generated by its longer predecessor.

The key change was a new section of tarmac linking the high-speed section beyond Eau Rouge with the return leg of the old track at Blanchimont. Yet the circuit retained the tight La Source hairpin that precedes the spectacular plunge down the hill towards the climbing Eau Rouge right-hander, which calls for considerable commitment and absolute precision from the competing drivers and is one of the most challenging corners on any circuit in the world.

The start/finish line had originally been positioned on this downhill section before Eau Rouge, but both the pits and starting grid were now repositioned on the short straight before the La Source hairpin from 1983 onwards. This presented the drivers with another tricky challenge, with a full grid of Grand Prix cars starting the race with a short sprint away from the start line before having to brake hard for the hairpin. The inevitable crowding usually results in two or three cars being eliminated within yards of the start, but by the same token it also puts the onus on the competitors to display considerable self-discipline in a very tight situation.

After hurtling through Eau Rouge, the cars begin the long climb towards Les Combes, which is a 190-mph (306-kmph) uphill sprint. This ends with an overtaking opportunity going into a medium-speed right/left-hander for those who have managed to exit on to the preceding straight a fraction faster than the competitor immediately ahead of them.

ON EARTH AT WHICH TO DRIVE A FORMULA 1 CAR'

There follows a plunging downhill sequence of bends, with no real chances for passing, which brings the cars back on to the old circuit at the 160-mph (257-kmph) Blanchimont right-hander. Then it is hard on the throttle once more for the return run back towards the pit area where the right 'bus stop' chicane provides another opportunity for the brave to have a stab at overtaking.

In 1993, the Lotus driver Alessandro Zanardi was involved in a huge accident at Eau Rouge from which he was extremely fortunate to escape unscathed. His car slammed into the right-hand retaining wall at about 150mph (241kmph), exciting concerns among the drivers about the proximity of the barriers to the edge of the tarmac at this point on the circuit.

In 1994, the character of the circuit was changed considerably by the installation of a temporary chicane at the entrance to Eau Rouge. This was regarded as a necessary evil by most of the drivers, whose enthusiasm for this high-speed corner was understandably tempered by concerns for their own personal safety in a season that had already been marred by the fatal accidents to Ayrton Senna and Roland Ratzenberger at Imola three months earlier.

Happily, for 1995 the organizers substantially extended the run-off areas at Eau Rouge, which allowed the old corner configuration to be reinstated. The challenge to skill and car control was thus retained with a welcome safety margin added to cater for a loss of control or technical malfunction.

Senna's four consecutive victories served to set a new benchmark in terms of driving skill at Spa. Having previously won there for Lotus in 1985, the Brazilian was now firmly established as the most successful driver of all time on the Belgian circuit. Yet in 1992 victory fell to Michael Schumacher's Benetton, the young German thereby posting the first victory of a career that would see him establish himself as F1's leading exponent in the post-Senna era.

In 1993, Damon Hill scored a great win for Williams and followed that up with a another win the following year, albeit inherited after Schumacher was disqualified for a technical infringement. Michael got his own back in 1995 with a terrific victory in treacherous wet/dry conditions, racing through from 16th place on the grid to beat Hill fair and square, then rammed home his status by winning again in 1996 at the wheel of the Ferrari F310.

In 1997 Schumacher returned to score a repeat victory for Ferrari, but this time he had no opposition whatsoever, dominating the race virtually from the start on a treacherously slippery track surface in his Ferrari F310B. Second place fell to the brilliant young Italian Giancarlo Fisichella at the wheel of a Jordan-Peugeot, six years to the weekend after Jordan had given the unproven Michael Schumacher his maiden F1 outing at the wheel of one of their cars.

Jos Verstappen's Benetton leads the Sauber of Heinz-Harald Frantzen into the braking area for Les Combes – one of Spa's possible overtaking places – in the 1994 Belgian Grand Prix.

CIRCUIT NACIONALE DE MONZA, MILAN

CIRCUIT LENGTH:
3.585 miles (5.770km).
LAP RECORD:
Michael Schumacher
(3.0 Ferrari F310), 1m 26.110s,
149.891mph (241.226kmph).
Lap record established in 1996.

CIRCUIT ASSESSMENT by ALAIN PROST:

'A very tricky circuit where you need to have good, high-speed chassis balance for the very quick corners, and excellent, consistent handling to deal with the tight chicanes. Curva Grande must be one of the most satisfying corners to get right on any circuit in the world.'

Imola's Autodromo Dino e Enzo Ferrari may have the most famous name, but Monza remains the spiritual home of Italian motor racing. Elegantly sited within an historic royal park on the fringes of Milan, the Monza autodrome was constructed by the Milan Automobile Club in 1922. Legendary names, such as Felice Nazzaro and Vincenzo Lancia, attended the ground-breaking ceremony and the circuit proved to be a great success until 1928, when Emilio Materassi's Talbot swerved into the crowd, killing its driver and 27 spectators.

After this horrific accident the Italian Grand Prix did not return to Monza until 1931, and only two years later drivers were killed when they slid off the track on an oil slick. For the next few years the race organizers experimented with several modified track designs all representing a variation on the so-called 'road circuit' – which largely makes up the Monza track configuration used to this day – and the secondary banked circuit that was finally demolished

Johnny Herbert's Sauber leads the Ligier of Pedro Diniz into the fast Parabolica right-hander during the 1996 Italian Grand Prix.

ITALIAN GRAND PRIX CIRCUIT NACIONALE DE MONZA, MILAN

CIRCUIT LENGTH:
3.585 miles (5.770km)

◸ = mph

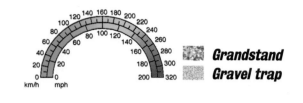

Grandstand
Gravel trap

Curva di Lesmo

Old abandoned banked circuit

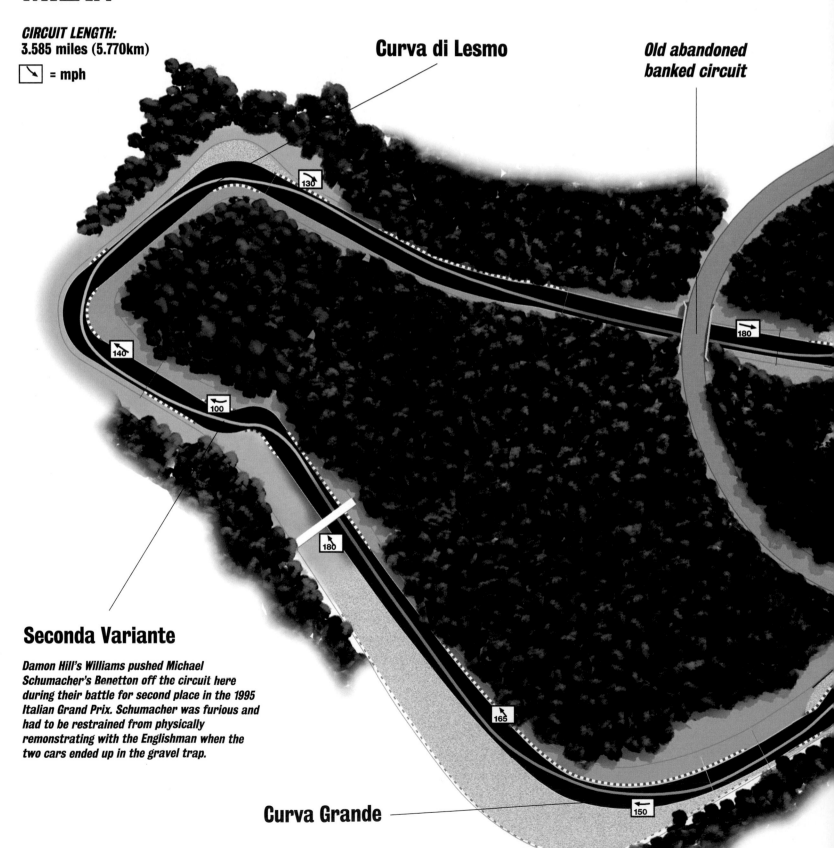

Seconda Variante

Damon Hill's Williams pushed Michael Schumacher's Benetton off the circuit here during their battle for second place in the 1995 Italian Grand Prix. Schumacher was furious and had to be restrained from physically remonstrating with the Englishman when the two cars ended up in the gravel trap.

Curva Grande

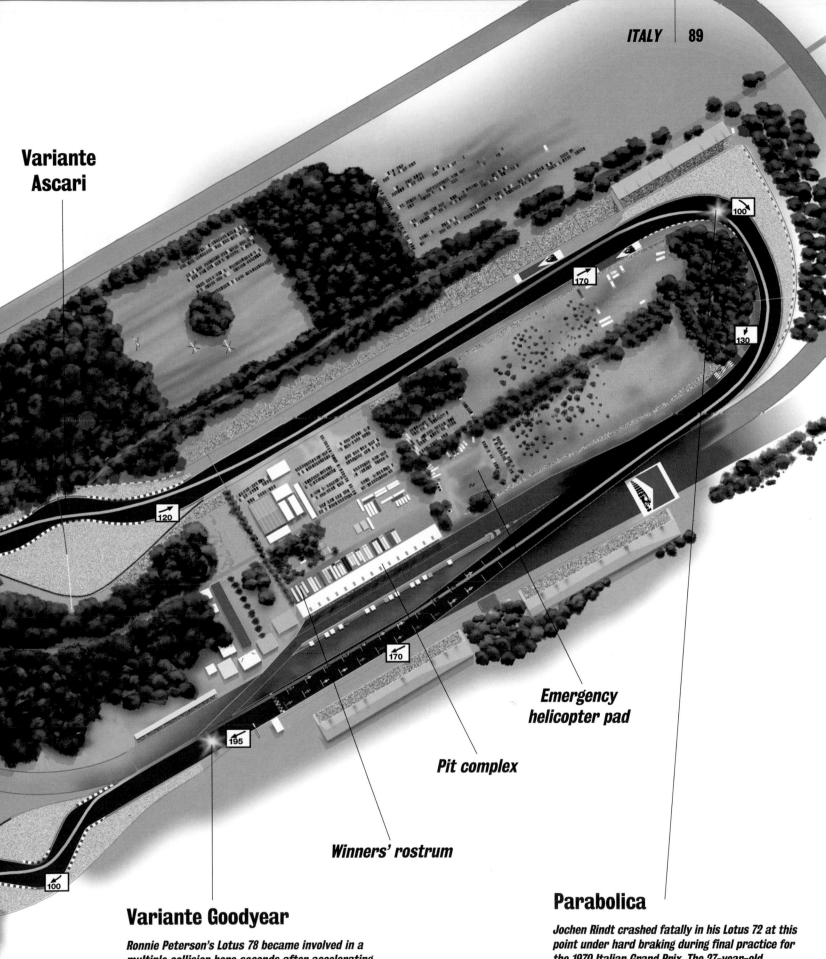

**Variante
Ascari**

**Emergency
helicopter pad**

Pit complex

Winners' rostrum

Variante Goodyear

Ronnie Peterson's Lotus 78 became involved in a
multiple collision here seconds after accelerating
away from the grid at the start of the 1978 Italian
Grand Prix. He subsequently died of complications
resulting from serious leg injuries.

Parabolica

Jochen Rindt crashed fatally in his Lotus 72 at this
point under hard braking during final practice for
the 1970 Italian Grand Prix. The 27-year-old
Austrian's Championship points lead was not
subsequently beaten, leaving him as the sport's
first – and so far only – posthumous title holder.

Just what the fans wanted. The Ferrari pit crew is jubilant as Michael Schumacher hurtles towards the chequered flag and victory on the last lap of the 1996 Italian Grand Prix at Monza.

shortly before the war, then rebuilt on a more extensive scale over the winter of 1954/55.

Thus the 1955 Italian Grand Prix took place over the combined road and banked circuit, the clever design of which meant that the competing cars passed down the main start/finish straight effectively twice a lap – although a single overall lap was judged to be one of the 3.9-mile (6.3-km) road circuit and one of the banking, a total of 6.2 miles (9.97km). It was a novel, mechanically bruising format that exacted a painful toll on the competing cars.

The combined banking and road circuit was also used, albeit in the reverse direction, for the incredible challenge races that were staged between European sports and F1 specials and a field of front-engined Indianapolis roadsters that came across from the USA for special guest appearances in 1957 and 1958.

These two events had the official title Race of the Two Worlds, although informally became known as the 'Monzanapolis' contests. Just to emphasize how fast a circuit Monza had become, visiting Indy driver Pat O'Connor completed a lap of the combined circuits at an average speed in excess of 170mph (274kmph) while conducting Firestone tyre tests prior to the 1958 event.

For the fearless Indianapolis drivers, Monza was just another race. However, many of the European competitors felt the whole thing to be unacceptably dangerous – a standpoint that was judged by some as being absolutely incredible at the time. Yet it was undeniable that the banked track represented an extremely precarious challenge for both driver and car. The Italian Grand Prix continued to be staged on the combined circuit format through to the end of 1961, after which it was abandoned for F1 cars although it did remain in use for international sports-car races right up until the end of the decade.

From 1962 onwards, the Italian GP settled down to be run on the road circuit alone. In those days it was unfettered by chicanes, and a daunting challenge

Von Trips' car was catapulted into the spectator retaining fence, killing not only its driver but also 13 onlookers in the crowd. Nine years later, at the very same point, World Championship points leader Jochen Rindt succumbed when his Lotus 72 crashed, almost certainly due to a brake-shaft failure, while qualifying for the 1970 Italian GP. Rindt became the sport's first posthumous title holder.

A year later, Britain's Peter Gethin drove a BRM to victory in the Italian GP by the closest-ever record-

'A VERY TRICKY CIRCUIT WITH TIGHT CHICANES'

saw cars bunched together in each other's slip-streams, running wheel to wheel at high speed.

The potential for catastrophe in such tight and difficult situations had already been devastatingly demonstrated in the 1961 Italian GP, when Wolfgang von Trips' Ferrari collided with Jim Clark's Lotus while braking from high speed for the tricky Parabolica turn, a 180-degree right-hander that leads the cars out on to the start/finish straight.

ed margin of one-hundredth of a second over Ronnie Peterson's March. Gethin's winning average speed of just over 150mph (241.4kmph) was also a record, testifying to the flat-out nature of the Monza challenge. Yet this was to be the penultimate slip-streaming epic at the famous Italian track. In the interests of safety, the circuit was slowed down by chicanes of varying severity from 1973 onwards, and steadily evolved into its current configuration.

Ukyo Katayama's Tyrrell brakes for the Lesmo right-hander during the 1996 Italian Grand Prix. Many of the trackside trees have been sacrificed to circuit safety improvements over the past two years.

In 1978, Monza witnessed yet another fatality when Ronnie Peterson's Lotus 78 was involved in a multiple collision with several other cars as he accelerated away from the Grand Prix starting grid. Peterson was extricated from the car with badly broken legs, but he sadly died later that night of a bone-marrow embolism. As with Clark's involvement with von Trips in 1961 and Rindt's fatality in 1970, the Lotus team had now been touched by tragedy for the third time in 17 years.

Monza lost the Italian Grand Prix to Imola for 1980 due to the complexities of the country's long-established motor-racing politics. But Imola retained its fixture as the San Marino Grand Prix, allowing the Italian Grand Prix proper to return to Monza, where it remains to this day.

It is still one of the most difficult and spectacular of circuits on the F1 Championship programme. From the starting grid, the cars funnel to the left of the entrance to the long-abandoned banking and have to brake hard for a tight S-bend. Life can become very crowded here – just like the first-lap scramble into the La Source hairpin at Spa – and at the start of the 1996 race, Jacques Villeneuve found himself being squeezed so roughly by team-mate Damon Hill he felt he had no alternative but to leave the track and drive across the run-off, behind the temporary retaining wall of tyres, before rejoining on the exit of the corner. He was distinctly unamused.

The cars then storm round Curva Grande before braking for the Seconda Variante – the second chicane – where overtaking moves are possible, but difficult in the extreme. This was the point at which Damon Hill's Williams took Michael Schumacher's Benetton off into the gravel trap during their battle

The deliriously happy fans spill out on to the circuit in the wake of Michael Schumacher's 1996 Ferrari victory at Monza.

No room! Damon Hill has squeezed Jacques Villeneuve's sister Williams on to the grass going through the first chicane at Monza at the start of the 1996 Italian Grand Prix. Villeneuve, having gone behind the tyre barriers on the apex of the right turn, is about to rejoin just behind his team-mate.

for second place in the 1995 Italian Grand Prix. The German driver was another who failed to see the funny side of this episode!

The section of the circuit from Curva Grande around to the Lesmo right-hander used to be flanked by densely packed woodland. However, in the summer of 1995 the FIA, motor racing's governing body, insisted that the run-off areas should be dramatically increased. Amid outcry and a chorus of controversy from the conservationists, hundreds of trees were felled in order that Formula 1 racing could remain at the Monza circuit.

Beyond the Lesmo right-hander, the track plunges downhill slightly, weaves back under the old banking, and then continues into the medium-speed Variante Ascari, which is a sweeping left/right/left S-bend that leads down the long straight to Parabolica.

Overtaking is difficult in the extreme at Monza, unless you have a performance advantage over the car you are seeking to pass, in which case you may be able to squeeze ahead into the first chicane, into the reprofiled first Lesmo, or – taking your life in your hands – braking for Variante Ascari.

More likely, a race will be won or lost in the pits. In 1996, shrewd refuelling strategy enabled Michael Schumacher's Ferrari to leapfrog ahead of Jean Alesi's Benetton. Once ahead of his rival, the German ace was able to pull comfortably away. But boxed in behind the Benetton, he could do nothing but follow in the car's wheel tracks.

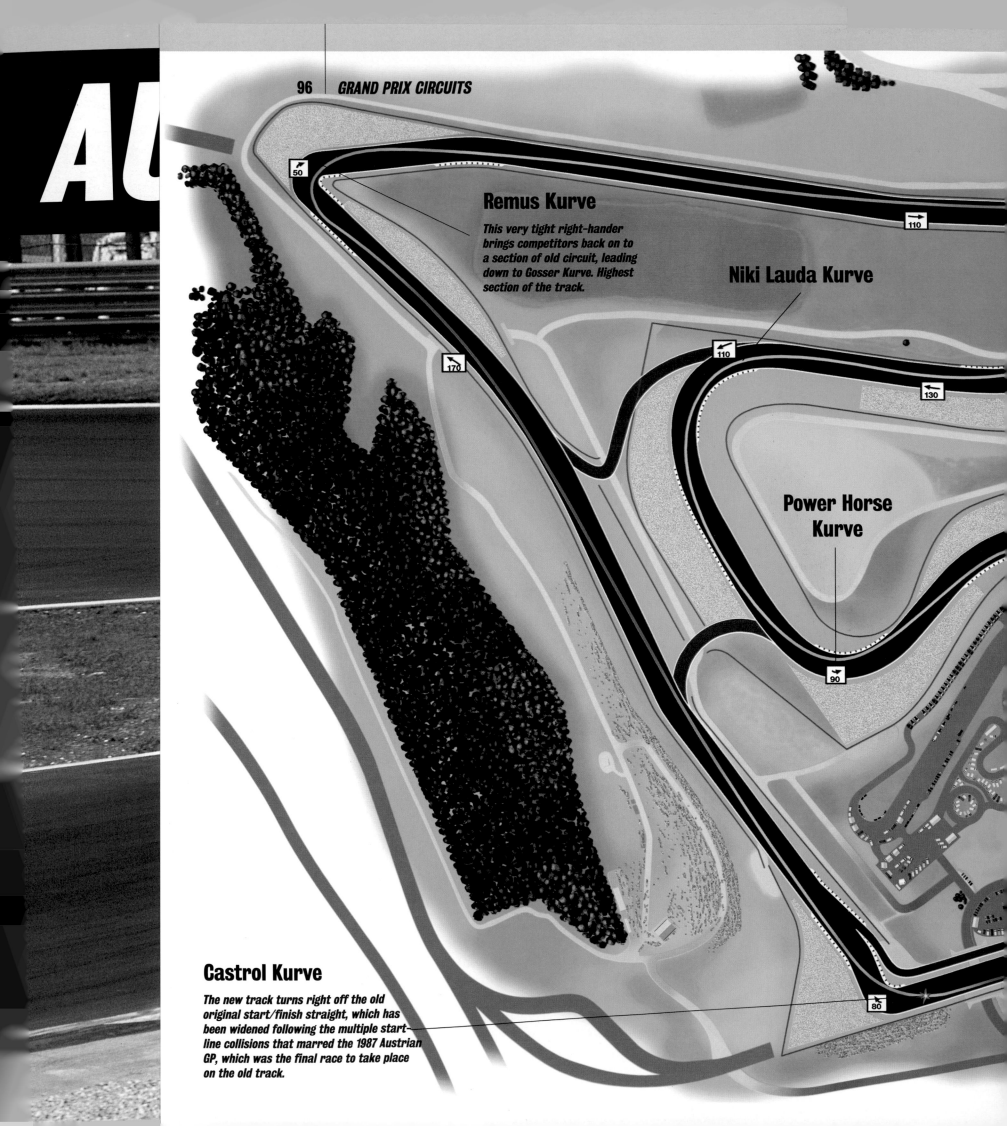

Remus Kurve

This very tight right-hander brings competitors back on to a section of old circuit, leading down to Gosser Kurve. Highest section of the track.

Niki Lauda Kurve

Power Horse Kurve

Castrol Kurve

The new track turns right off the old original start/finish straight, which has been widened following the multiple start-line collisions that marred the 1987 Austrian GP, which was the final race to take place on the old track.

50

110

170

110

130

90

80

AUSTRIAN GRAND PRIX
A1-RING, NEAR KNITTELFELD

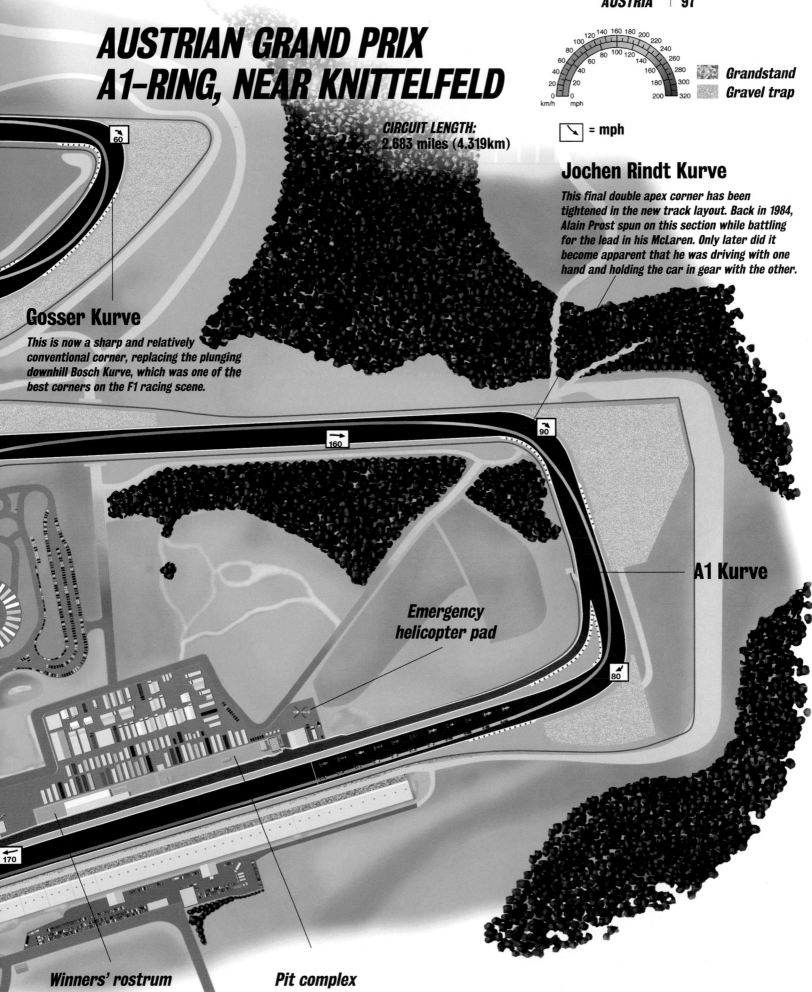

CIRCUIT LENGTH:
2.683 miles (4.319km)

Grandstand
Gravel trap

= mph

Jochen Rindt Kurve

This final double apex corner has been tightened in the new track layout. Back in 1984, Alain Prost spun on this section while battling for the lead in his McLaren. Only later did it become apparent that he was driving with one hand and holding the car in gear with the other.

Gosser Kurve

This is now a sharp and relatively conventional corner, replacing the plunging downhill Bosch Kurve, which was one of the best corners on the F1 racing scene.

A1 Kurve

Emergency helicopter pad

Winners' rostrum

Pit complex

Nigel Mansell hurtles towards the Boschkurve en route to victory in the 1987 Austrian Grand Prix. The new circuit will be significantly less spectacular than its predecessor.

pressures resulted in the circuit being closed for international events from 1988 onwards.

Safety was always going to be a potential problem on a circuit with so many high-speed corners, particularly when the run-off areas consisted in the main of little more than vast expanses of greensward. During the race morning warm-up for the 1975 Austrian Grand Prix, the American driver and Indy 500 winner Mark Donohue crashed his March 751 at the Hella Licht curve at the top of the hill beyond the pits, sustaining serious head injuries from which he subsequently died.

This resulted in a chicane being installed at that point on the circuit, but otherwise the track remained pretty well unchanged right through to the final race in 1987. Another problem was the very confined start/finish section that ran between the vertical walls of the pit front and the spectator area, without any run-offs whatsoever. Two multiple collisions on the starting grid resulted in the 1987 race getting underway only at its third attempt. You could say that this was the last straw for the classic Österreichring.

The advent of the Hungarian Grand Prix seemed to suppress any possibility of Austria regaining its status in the ranks of F1 host countries. Eventually, in 1986, the track was revamped and revised to the point that it could no longer be regarded as having much to do with the old facility that had become a part of Grand Prix folklore. The A1-Ring, as it is now called, is scheduled to revive the Austrian GP in 1997. It may be in the same place as the Österreichring, but the signs are that it is not a shadow of its former self.

triumphed at the wheel of a BRM P160, and then it was Emerson Fittipaldi's turn to give Lotus their first Austrian Formula 1 success in the following year.

For 18 years, the Österreichring occupied a majestic position on the F1 calendar, regarded by many people as absolutely the best circuit in the world. However, increasing safety concerns – Nigel Mansell won the 1987 Austrian GP at an average speed of 150mph (241.4kmph) – and commercial

'PASSING WILL BE VERY DIFFICULT WHEN

Accelerating away from the start/finish line, there is a short climb before the track goes right, about 218 yards (200m) before the old Hella Licht chicane. That is followed by a steady uphill climb to a tight right-hander with a steepening entry. This is quite slow and, as 1976 Austrian Grand Prix winner, John Watson, discovered when he tested a 1996 Sauber-Ford Formula 1 car at the new track shortly after its completion, it can be taken in first gear.

The track then goes downhill along a fast straight to the site of the former Boschkurve, once a daunting 180-degree, plunging right-hander. This has been slowed considerably, but the next two left-handers have at least retained some of their previous character.

The crest before the final right-hander – still happily named the Rindt Kurve – has been flattened slightly, and this is approached at about 175mph (282kmph).

This in turn brings the cars around through almost 180 degrees and catapults them out down a gentle hill towards the start/finish line. In Watson's estimation, there are about three possible overtaking points on the new A1-Ring. The track is a pale shadow of the old Österreichring, yet Austrian Formula 1 fans will just be thankful that they have regained their foothold on the Grand Prix business. For a country that produced F1 talents of the calibre of Jochen Rindt, Niki Lauda and Gerhard Berger, they probably deserve it more than most.

Epic backdrop, but the new A1-Ring projects a somewhat bland character.

THE RACE EVENTUALLY COMES HERE'

LUXEMBOURG

NÜRBURGRING, NEAR KOBLENZ

CIRCUIT LENGTH:
2.831 miles (4.556km).
LAP RECORD:
Michael Schumacher
(3.0 Benetton-Renault B195), 1m 21.180s,
125.540mph (202.039kmph).
Lap record established in 1995.

CIRCUIT ASSESSMENT by DAMON HILL:

'A circuit where you have to be precise, and it is also deceptively quick. You have to judge your overtaking opportunities very precisely while at the same time trying not to get too far out of line in the traffic. It is a track I quite enjoy.'

THE START/FINISH STRAIGHT OF THE NEW NÜRBURGRING IS THE ONLY SECTION OF THE TRACK THAT EFFECTIVELY RUNS ALONG THE PATH OF THE OLD 14-MILE (22.5-KM) CIRCUIT THROUGH THE EIFEL MOUNTAINS, ON WHICH SO MUCH GRAND PRIX HISTORY WAS WRITTEN.

The contrast between the two courses is stark, emphasizing just how much motor racing has changed and evolved during the post-war years. From the back of the paddock, the old Nürburgring can be seen wending its tortuous and bumpy path into the distance through the forests. But the existing track is bland, modern and lined with wide run-offs. The new Nürburgring has so far hosted only four rounds of the FIA Formula 1 World Championship. These have been the 1984, 1995 and 1996 European Grands Prix and the 1985 German Grand Prix.

The story of the new Nürburgring can have no meaning unless one considers the history of the original circuit. The concept of a race track in the Eifel mountains had been originally mooted before the First World War, but it was not until the early 1920s that the idea began to take on a serious focus. One of the driving forces behind the track, which would come to be called the Nürburgring, was a local-government politician, then the mayor of nearby

Jacques Villeneuve's Williams leads David Coulthard's McLaren and the rest of the field into the fast S-bend beyond the pits at Nürburgring at the start of the 1996 European Grand Prix.

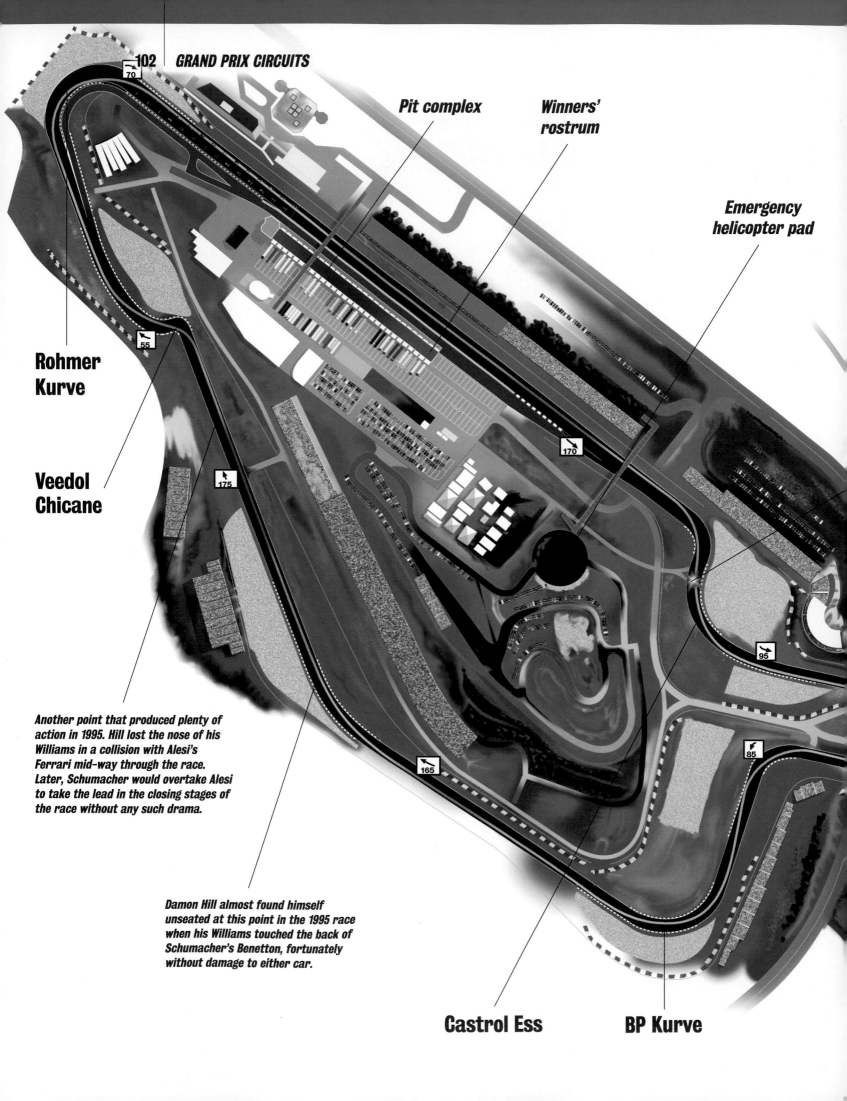

Pit complex

Winners'
rostrum

Emergency
helicopter pad

**Rohmer
Kurve**

**Veedol
Chicane**

*Another point that produced plenty of
action in 1995. Hill lost the nose of his
Williams in a collision with Alesi's
Ferrari mid-way through the race.
Later, Schumacher would overtake Alesi
to take the lead in the closing stages of
the race without any such drama.*

*Damon Hill almost found himself
unseated at this point in the 1995 race
when his Williams touched the back of
Schumacher's Benetton, fortunately
without damage to either car.*

Castrol Ess

BP Kurve

LUXEMBOURG GRAND PRIX NÜRBURGRING, NEAR KOBLENZ

CIRCUIT LENGTH:
2.831 miles (4.556km)

 = mph

David Coulthard's McLaren edged ahead of Jacques Villeneuve's Williams on the sprint towards this corner on the opening lap of the 1996 European GP, but Villeneuve had the inside line and kept his advantage. Back in 1984, this corner saw a multiple pile-up triggered by a collision between new boy Ayrton Senna's Toleman and Keke Rosberg's Williams.

Tricky downhill braking on the approach to this corner makes for a particularly difficult section of the circuit. This is where Schumacher's Ferrari got within feet of Villeneuve's winning Williams during their battle for the lead in 1996.

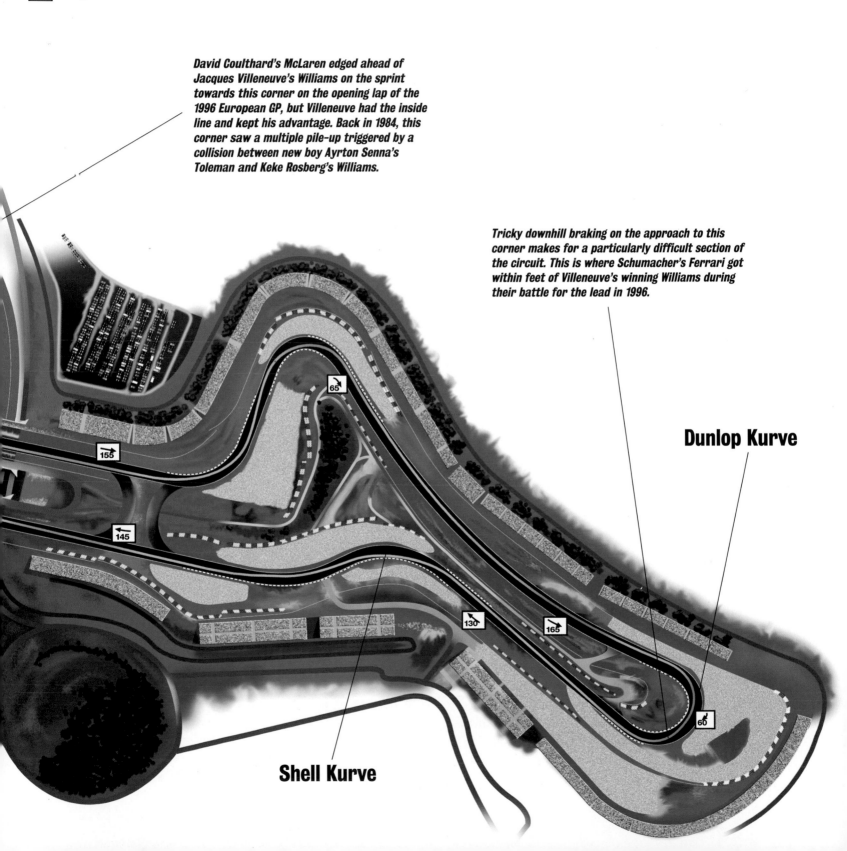

Dunlop Kurve

Shell Kurve

Mika Salo rides his Tyrrell high over the kerb on the tight chicane just before the pits at Nürburgring, one of the circuit's overtaking opportunities.

Cologne, Konrad Adenauer. Adenauer was later to become Chancellor of West Germany.

The intention behind the Nürburgring was that it would be used as a test track for the German motor industry, while at the same time the intensive labour required for its construction would go some way towards alleviating the high levels of unemployment in this rural area. Construction of the circuit began in April 1925 and the first race was held in front of 150,000 spectators on 18 June 1927.

The inaugural race was won by Rudolf Caracciola behind the wheel of an S-type Mercedes-Benz. It could hardly have been a more appropriate victory, for Caracciola would go on to establish a reputation as one of the greatest German racing drivers of all time. At the same time, the drivers would come to regard the challenging 14-mile (22.5-km) Nürburgring as one of the most demanding race tracks in the world – a suitable venue for the Nazi regime to demonstrate the superiority of its Mercedes

and Auto-Union products in the decade running up to the outbreak of the Second World War.

Of course, Nürburgring was a circuit on which driver virtuosity could frequently compensate for any performance deficit on the part of the cars. In 1935, the legendary Tazio Nuvolari's outclassed Alfa Romeo trounced the might of the German teams. Nobody had expected such an outlandish result and there was no recording of the Italian national anthem with which to salute the victor. Nuvolari came to their rescue; he always carried such a record around with him. Just in case!

Twenty-six years later, Stirling Moss drove his Rob Walker team four-cylinder Lotus 18 to a similarly outstanding victory over the more powerful Ferrari V6s in the 1961 German Grand Prix. Jackie Stewart won brilliantly in rain and fog seven years later, but then Niki Lauda's fiery accident at the wheel of a Ferrari in 1976 finally sounded the old Nürburgring's death knell.

The German Grand Prix was moved to Hockenheim, but pressure remained to somehow continue racing at the Nürburgring. There was obviously no question of updating the old 14-mile (22.5-km) circuit to meet contemporary safety standards – that would have been prohibitively expensive – so it was decided to construct a brand new circuit. This was duly completed, and the new Nürburgring hosted the European Grand Prix for the first time in 1984 as the penultimate round of the World Championship competition battle.

By this stage in the season, McLaren team-mates Alain Prost and Niki Lauda were locked firmly into an internecine battle for the title. Prost, by now, seemingly had the upper hand, and while the Frenchman romped away to win the race, Lauda wound up a disappointed fourth, having been pitched into a spin as he came up to lap the slow Spirit-Hart driven by the Italian Mauro Baldi.

In fact, this incident had been Lauda's fault, yet after the race he decided to go and give Baldi a verbal battering, presumably on the basis that the senior driver naturally assumes precedence. But Niki had not banked on the feisty little Italian's response. Baldi rounded on him, told him not to be so bloody stupid and that the whole episode had been nobody's fault but Lauda's. Exit the McLaren driver from the fray, looking slightly puzzled.

In 1985, the German Grand Prix saw Prost's McLaren beaten by Michele Alboreto's Ferrari, after which ten years passed before the F1 fraternity returned to the Nürburgring to see Michael Schumacher win convincingly for Benetton, while Damon Hill's Williams spun off the circuit.

In that race, Schumacher could have settled for second place, but threw caution to the wind and overtook Jean Alesi's Ferrari for the lead in the closing stages of the race. Interestingly, that ten-year gap between the 1985 and 1995 races produced a dramatic change in the perception of the new Nürburgring. At first glance it had been dismissed as a featureless, slightly bland autodrome. By 1995, the new generation of Grand Prix drivers judged it 'not bad at all'.

Accelerating away from the starting grid, the track slopes away gently as the cars approach the Castrol Ess, a tricky S-bend under braking for which there are opportunities for overtaking on a flying lap, but not when approached from the grid after a standing start. The track then runs downhill through a left/right sequence of turns to the Dunlop Kurve, which marks the lowest point on the track, a wide, 180-degree corner that is touch-and-go for considering any type of passing manoeuvre.

Then comes a long haul back uphill through the fast left-hand Shell Kurve through to the right-hand BP Kurve, followed by a fast right-hander leading down to the Veedol chicane and then the final, uphill right-hand, Rohmer Kurve, which leads out on to the start/finish straight. Generally, overtaking is quite difficult at the Nürburgring, although Schumacher, in particular, has managed to elbow past opposition going into the Veedol chicane – but only with a degree of acquiescence from his immediate rival.

The 1996 European Grand Prix saw a particularly close-fought battle between Jacques Villeneuve's Williams – heading for the Canadian driver's maiden F1 win – and Schumacher's Ferrari. It was a terrific performance by Villeneuve to resist what seemed at one point like overwhelming pressure from the German on his home territory, but the new boy was not to be flustered. It was one of the best races yet seen on this new circuit, a contest that went some way to keep alive the epic traditions of the old, by now long-discarded, Nürburgring.

A general view of the lower end of the circuit, with the wide, sweeping Dunlop Kurve. The cars in the foreground are negotiating the Shell Kurve.

SUZUKA SPEEDWAY, NEAR NAGOYA

CIRCUIT LENGTH:
3.644 miles (5.864km).
LAP RECORD:
Nigel Mansell
(3.5 Williams-Renault FW14B), 1m 40.646s,
130.332mph (207.749kmph).
Lap record established in 1992.

CIRCUIT ASSESSMENT by UKYO KATAYAMA:

'Hard on the tyres, Suzuka offers a longer-than-average lap, which makes for exciting racing. It doesn't provide many places to pass, however, and you have to display split-second judgement to overtake at the chicane before the pits. A special place for me, obviously.'

THE SUZUKA CIRCUIT WAS ORIGINALLY CONSTRUCTED IN 1962. IT WAS USED AS A TEST TRACK BY HONDA FOR MANY YEARS AS WELL AS STAGING A LARGE NUMBER OF NATIONAL-LEVEL RACE MEETINGS. IN 1976, JAPAN HOSTED ITS FIRST WORLD CHAMPIONSHIP GRAND PRIX AT THE MOUNT FUJI CIRCUIT, REPEATING THIS FIXTURE IN 1977 BEFORE THE RACE WAS DROPPED FROM THE CALENDAR FOR A PERIOD OF TEN YEARS. IT RESURFACED AT SUZUKA IN 1987, BY WHICH TIME THE CIRCUIT NEAR NAGOYA HAD BEEN EXTENSIVELY UPDATED TO CONFORM WITH CONTEMPORARY SAFETY REQUIREMENTS.

The circuit layout at Suzuka is distinctive and unusual in that it doubles back on itself in a figure-of-eight configuration. It is also slightly longer than a typical contemporary Grand Prix circuit, which means that competing drivers have to concentrate on conserving tyre performance for maximum grip, particularly during qualifying runs.

Japan's motor-racing heritage has been shaped only recently, within the time span of Suzuka's

Suzuka has just one serious place to overtake – into the tight chicane by the pits, just out of sight past the fast right-hander where a Ligier (parked to the left) has shed its wing in the middle of the circuit.

Hairpin

Spoon Curve

Into this gravel trap spun Damon Hill's Williams to end his disappointing 1995 race at Suzuka after a performance that many believe convinced Frank Williams to replace him with Heinz-Harald Frentzen for 1997.

130R

The scene of a particularly unpleasant high-speed accident to Mark Blundell's McLaren during practice for the 1995 race. He recovered magnificently to climb through from last on the starting grid to seventh place in the following day's race.

Degner Curve

CIRCUIT LENGTH:
3.644 miles (5.864km)

= mph

JAPANESE GRAND PRIX SUZUKA SPEEDWAY, NEAR NAGOYA

120 140 160 180 200
100   220
80   240
60   260
40   280
20   300
0   320
km/h   mph

Grandstand
Gravel trap

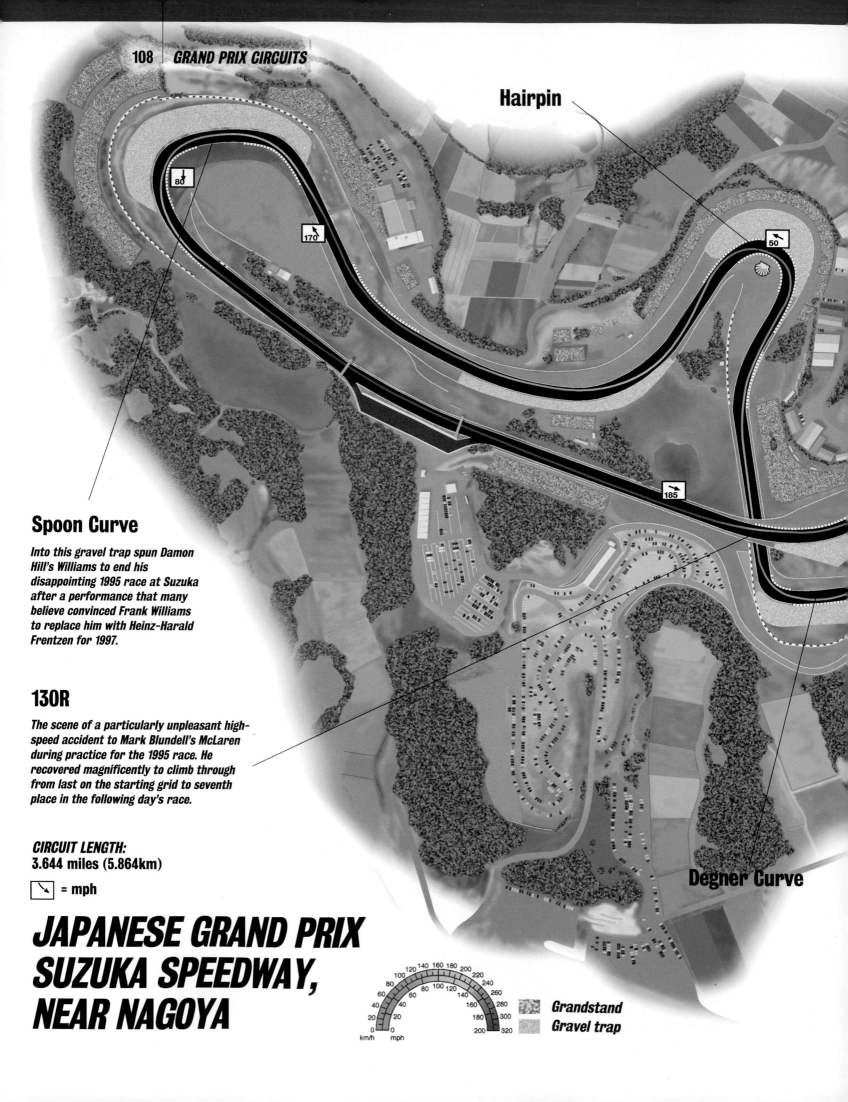

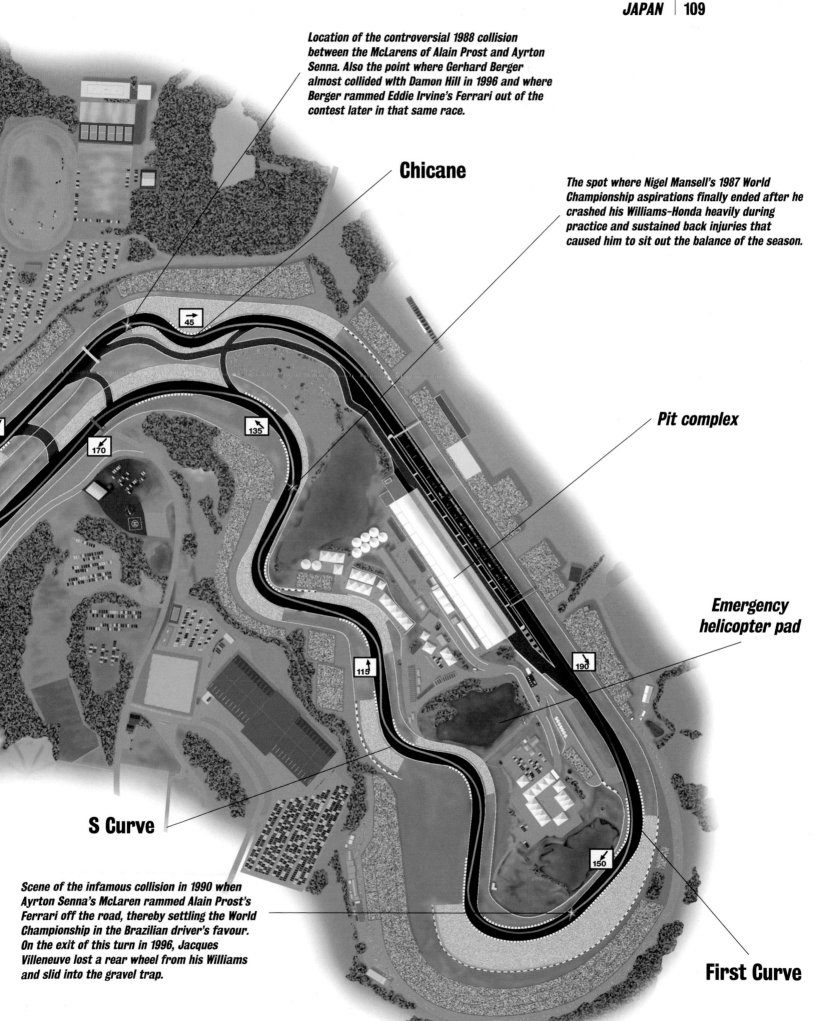

Location of the controversial 1988 collision between the McLarens of Alain Prost and Ayrton Senna. Also the point where Gerhard Berger almost collided with Damon Hill in 1996 and where Berger rammed Eddie Irvine's Ferrari out of the contest later in that same race.

Chicane

The spot where Nigel Mansell's 1987 World Championship aspirations finally ended after he crashed his Williams-Honda heavily during practice and sustained back injuries that caused him to sit out the balance of the season.

Pit complex

Emergency helicopter pad

S Curve

Scene of the infamous collision in 1990 when Ayrton Senna's McLaren rammed Alain Prost's Ferrari off the road, thereby settling the World Championship in the Brazilian driver's favour. On the exit of this turn in 1996, Jacques Villeneuve lost a rear wheel from his Williams and slid into the gravel trap.

First Curve

Gerhard Berger's McLaren and Stefano Modena's Brabham sit stranded in the gravel trap on the outside of the first corner at Suzuka, following their spins during the 1990 Japanese Grand Prix.

'SUZUKA OFFERS A LONGER-THAN-AVERAGE

existence. In the early days, the track was used for motorcycle testing as well as evaluating Honda's first 1.5-litre Grand Prix car, which made its Formula 1 debut in the 1964 German Grand Prix. At the time, this creation was regarded with a sense of indulgent amusement by the European motor-racing community, but with the passage of another 20 years Japan would be firmly established as a leading player in this colourful, high-technology sport.

By the time the Japanese Grand Prix was first staged at Suzuka in 1987, the World Championship battle was finely balanced between Williams-Honda team-mates Nigel Mansell and Nelson Piquet. Battling for the fastest time in qualifying, Mansell spun off and crashed heavily on the fast S-bends behind the paddock. Although the team repaired and fettled his car for the following day's practice session, Mansell, who had been briefly held in hospital,

discharged himself and returned to Europe suffering from back injuries.

The result of his departure was to present Piquet with the third World Championship crown of his career, although he retired in the race itself, which was won in commanding fashion by Berger's Ferrari ahead of Senna's Lotus-Honda.

In 1988, an all-McLaren-Honda battle for the Championship title between team-mates Senna and Alain Prost resulted in a terrific battle at Suzuka, with Senna climbing back through the field after almost stalling at the start to take the first of his three titles with a magnificent victory.

Somehow, the Suzuka circuit configuration inevitably produced good, close racing at the Japanese Grand Prix, but never more so than in 1989 when Prost and Senna were pitched against each other for the final time as McLaren team-mates.

LAP, WHICH MAKES FOR EXCITING RACING'

Prost made a slight aerodynamic change to his car's set-up on the starting grid and this endowed it with a fraction more straight-line speed than was available for his rival's machine.

This change enabled Prost to get away ahead, leaving the capacity crowd absolutely spellbound as Senna strained every sinew to get on terms with the Frenchman. It looked like stalemate, but with the World Championship at stake, Senna would not give up. He finally took a deep breath, hung tight on to Prost's tail coming through the flat-out 130R left-hander before the pits and then level in an attempt to outbrake Prost into the punishingly tight chicane by the start/finish line.

This point on the circuit was widely regarded as offering the only realistic overtaking opportunity, but the success of Senna's challenge depended on Prost being compliant. With the Championship hanging in the balance between the two men, Prost was far from that, and he duly closed the door. The two McLarens colliding and skidding to a halt, locked together, in the middle of the chicane.

Prost, confident that the World Championship was his, undid his belts and climbed out. Senna, never one to give up on a challenge, beckoned the marshals to help him restart and chased off once again. Despite a pit stop to fit a replacement nose section, he managed to catch and pass Alessandro Nannini's Benetton to be first past the chequered flag. He was then disqualified from the race for negotiating the chicane incorrectly when he went to rejoin the race. Nannini was awarded the win.

This exclusion from the race was directly responsible for Senna's failure to win the 1990 World Championship, interrupting a sequence of success that would have otherwise seen him win four titles before his death at Imola in 1994. The Brazilian driver smouldered with indignation, both at Prost and the sport's governing body, whom he clearly felt were in league together, plotting against his interests.

A year later, Suzuka was the scene of one of the most remarkable accidents in motor-racing history. Prost, by now driving for Ferrari, had to win the Japanese Grand Prix to retain an outside chance of winning the Championship title. Yet his chance was snatched away on the very first corner where Senna simply rammed him off the road into the gravel trap at 120mph (193kmph).

Legacy of a disaster. Ayrton Senna's McLaren and Alain Prost's Ferrari lie nose-to-nose in the Suzuka gravel trap after Senna deliberately pushed Prost off the road at the first corner of the 1990 race.

This display was a chilling example of Ayrton Senna's absolute self-belief, which took no account of the fact that he pulled this potentially suicidal move ahead of a packed field of 22 other cars. Mercifully, the wrecked McLaren and Ferrari spun off on to the wide gravel trap on the outside of the appropriately titled First Curve. Senna had been annoyed by the organizers' unwillingness to let him start from pole position on the clean outside line – and he exacted his revenge, on the system and his rival, with deadly precision.

Ironically, 12 months later, Senna displayed a completely different facet of his character – again at Suzuka. Having been supported ably and loyally by his new McLaren team-mate, Gerhard Berger, throughout the season, Ayrton slowed up coming out of the final chicane on the last lap to let his Austrian friend win the Japanese Grand Prix. Senna clearly felt that it was enough to have been crowned World Champion for a third time.

In 1992, Nigel Mansell extended the same courtesy to his Williams-Renault team-mate, Riccardo Patrese, although the Englishman's engine failed after he allowed the Italian to take the lead. More fun and games were waiting in 1993 when Senna, leading the race in his McLaren-Ford, found cheeky new boy Eddie Irvine making a race of it as he came up to lap the Ulsterman's Jordan-Hart.

Senna was not even remotely amused, and the episode ended with punches thrown and insults traded in the paddock after the race. By the time it came to the 1994 Japanese Grand Prix, Senna was no longer alive and it was Damon Hill who scored a brilliant victory in pouring rain for Williams, winning ahead of Michael Schumacher's Benetton.

Schumacher repaid the compliment in 1995, but Hill scored a glorious victory in 1996 when he led from start to finish to clinch his World Championship. He knew that he would have to get away cleanly at the start, and did just that, leaving his team-mate Jacques Villeneuve – the only other title contender – bogged down in traffic during the early stages of the race.

Suzuka is a strange circuit inasmuch as it often produces close racing with little overtaking opportunities. The chicane before the pits is the crucial section of the circuit in this respect, but, like Senna did in 1989, a driver has to come through the 130R left-hander a tad quicker than his opponent ahead – and then brake incredibly late – if he is to have a chance of making a place.

Nelson Piquet and Roberto Moreno line astern in their Benetton–Fords lead a gaggle of cars down the Suzuka start-line straight en route to a 1-2 finish after Senna, Prost and Berger all left the road.

SPAIN

CIRCUITO DE JEREZ

CIRCUIT LENGTH:
2.751 miles (4.428km)
LAP RECORD:
Michael Schumacher
(3.5 Benetton-Ford B194), 1m 25.040s,
116.429mph(187.4450kmh).
Lap record established in 1994.

CIRCUIT ASSESSMENT by JOHNNY HERBERT:

'Jerez can be quite a frustrating circuit, because if the guy in front of you is going slightly slower, there are precious few opportunities to overtake unless he feels willing to oblige. The track surface also gets quite dirty off the racing line, which inevitably adds to the challenge. Getting a clean run into the first corner after the pits offers the best chance of overtaking.'

THE SPANISH GRAND PRIX HAS TENDED TOWARDS A SOMEWHAT NOMADIC EXISTENCE SINCE THE EARLY YEARS OF THE OFFICIAL WORLD CHAMPIONSHIP. THE RACE INITIALLY TOOK PLACE ON BARCELONA'S PEDRALBES STREET ROAD CIRCUIT UNTIL 1954, AFTER WHICH TIME THERE WAS A 14-YEAR INTERREGNUM UNTIL THE RACE RETURNED TO THE GRAND PRIX CALENDAR AT MADRID'S JARAMA TRACK, THEN REGARDED AS SOMETHING OF AN ANTISEPTIC AND SANITIZED MODERN 'FACILITY'.

From 1969 onwards, Jarama alternated the race with Barcelona's spectacular Montjuich Park circuit, but a serious accident resulting in the deaths of four onlookers, when German driver Rolf Stommelen's car plunged into the crowd, resulted in Montjuich being abandoned for international racing.

Jarama then retained the Spanish GP through to 1981, after which it lapsed from the calendar. It was eventually revived in 1986 on a newly built circuit at

Jerez saw the closest finish in GP history in 1986, when Ayrton Senna's Lotus 98T (left) just pipped Nigel Mansell's Williams FW11 to win the race by one-thousandth of a second.

Practice for the 1998 Spanish Grand Prix was marred by a 140-mph (225-kmph) accident involving Martin Donnelly's Lotus-Lamborghini which suffered a technical failure and slammed into the barrier at this point. The front of the car disintegrated and Donnelly was hurled out onto the track, still strapped to his seat. Badly injured, he took a year to recover from multiple injuries, but never managed to resume his Grand Prix career.

EUROPEAN GRAND PRIX
CIRCUITO DE JEREZ

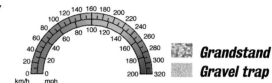

Grandstand
Gravel trap

CIRCUIT LENGTH:
2.751 miles (4.428km)

◥ = mph

Pit complex

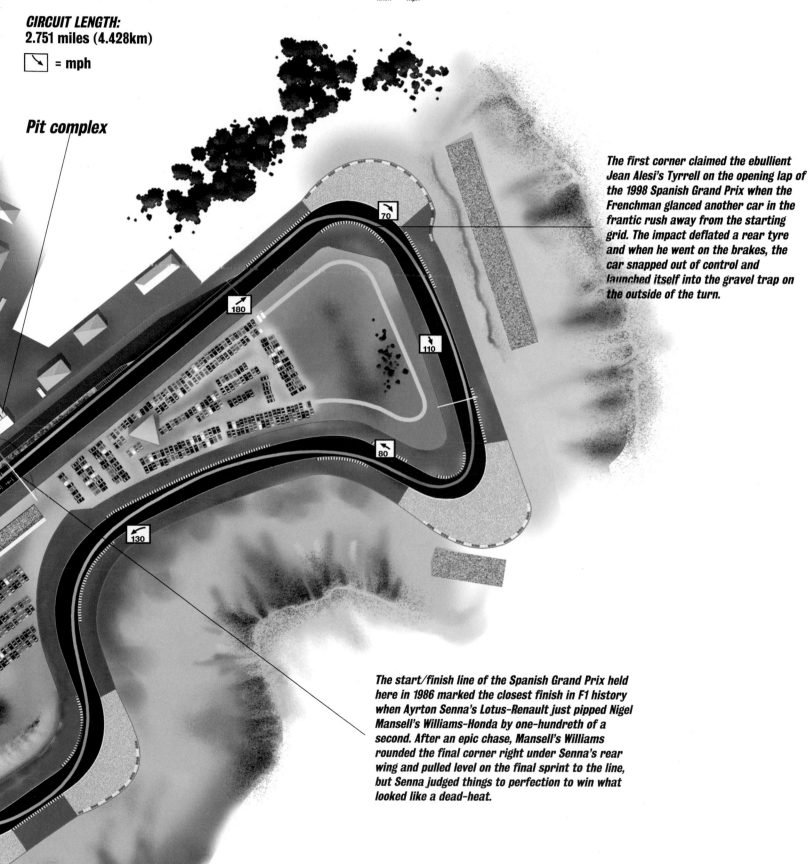

The first corner claimed the ebullient Jean Alesi's Tyrrell on the opening lap of the 1998 Spanish Grand Prix when the Frenchman glanced another car in the frantic rush away from the starting grid. The impact deflated a rear tyre and when he went on the brakes, the car snapped out of control and launched itself into the gravel trap on the outside of the turn.

The start/finish line of the Spanish Grand Prix held here in 1986 marked the closest finish in F1 history when Ayrton Senna's Lotus-Renault just pipped Nigel Mansell's Williams-Honda by one-hundreth of a second. After an epic chase, Mansell's Williams rounded the final corner right under Senna's rear wing and pulled level on the final sprint to the line, but Senna judged things to perfection to win what looked like a dead-heat.

The start of the 1990 Spanish GP with Ayrton Senna's McLaren-Honda (no 27) just reaching the first corner ahead of the reigning World Champion Alain Prost in a Ferrari and the rest of the pack. On the far right, Jan Alesi's Tyrrell is riding the outside kerb and is about to spin off into the gravel trap.

Jerez de la Frontera, in the heart of Spain's sherry-producing countryside.

The track was quite tight and undramatic, rated as moderately interesting by most of the drivers. Yet the inaugural Spanish GP to be staged there proved to be one of the very best F1 races of the decade.

Ayrton Senna was by now firmly established as the number one driver in the Lotus-Renault team. The Brazilian driver's performances in qualifying were simply awesome and the team had developed a very effective chassis set-up for the new Lotus 98T, which enabled him to maximize his potential in the battle for grid positions.

So it proved at Jerez, where Senna qualified on pole position ahead of his compatriot Nelson Piquet in a Williams-Honda, while the second row was occupied by Nigel Mansell's Williams-Honda and the McLaren-TAG driven by the reigning World Champion, Alain Prost.

Senna's reputation for faultless starts remained intact as the Lotus sprinted ahead into the first corner, chased by Piquet, Mansell, Keke Rosberg's McLaren and Prost. Ayrton was prudently running only as quickly as his fuel-consumption read-out would allow. F1 regulations at the time permitted a maximum tank capacity of 195 litres (42.89 gallons) – and no refuelling was permitted.

Despite Senna's prowess, Mansell caught and passed the leading Lotus and the contest quickly developed into a two-horse race. Remorselessly, the Englishman extended his advantage, but just as it looked as though he had his first win of the 1986 firmly in his grasp, he suddenly began to appreciate that he was in potential trouble as the rear end of his car began to slide about all over the circuit.

The rear aerodynamic diffuser panel, which affects the critical airflow beneath the car, had become damaged – a rear tyre had somehow picked up some debris and he was now grappling with a slow puncture.

Mid-way round lap 62 – with just ten left to run – Senna came through in the lead ahead of Prost's McLaren as Mansell headed for the pit lane to fit fresh tyres. A matter of seconds later, the Williams erupted from the pit lane like a dragster.

Senna was now almost 20 seconds ahead, but what followed was a simply explosive performance by the British driver. The Williams-Honda destroyed the Lotus's advantage, the gap tumbling on consecutive laps: 15.3 seconds, 12.8 seconds, 8.7 seconds. Then he caught Prost and lost a few fractions as he overtook the McLaren.

The odds still seemed impossible. With two laps to go he was 5.3 seconds down, then next time around he sliced an unbelievable 3.8 seconds off Ayrton's advantage. He went into the final lap just 1.5 seconds adrift and the two cars sprinted under the chequered winner's flag just one-thousandth of a second apart.

Mansell would return twelve months later to win the 1987 race commandingly for the Williams-Honda squad, but in 1988 it was Prost's McLaren that beat him into second place. Senna won in 1989, but practice for the 1990 race was marred by a terrible accident to Martin Donnelly, who was left lying in the middle of the track strapped to his seat after his Lotus literally disintegrated after smashing heavily into a guard rail.

Donnelly was critically injured in the crash, although thankfully he pulled through. His recovery took the best part of a year, but his professional racing career was over. Prost won the race from Mansell, both men driving Ferraris now, while Mansell returned to Williams to win again the following year, although by now political considerations meant that the race was transferred to the brand-new Circuit de Catalunya at Barcelona.

Four years would lapse before Jerez again hosted a World Championship Grand Prix nearing the end of the 1994 F1 season. By then Ayrton Senna, the winner of that magical first race eight years before, would be dead, killed at the wheel of a Williams-Renault at Imola. It then fell to his team-mate

Damon Hill to carry aloft his fallen banner and to challenge the emergent Michael Schumacher for the World Championship.

The 1994 Jerez race took the title of European Grand Prix, Hill having earlier won the official Spanish race at the Circuit de Catalunya. Damon qualified second behind Schumacher's Benetton but surged into an immediate lead on the sprint to the first tricky uphill right-hander.

In the opening stages, the Williams and Benetton cars ran in close company, pulling away from the rest of the pack together, but Hill eventually lost valuable time due to a problem with his team's refuelling rig during one of his routine pit stops. It was a bitter blow, forcing him to settle for second place behind Schumacher as a result.

Jerez made yet another Formula 1 curtain call at the end of the 1997 racing season, this Cinderella of circuits taking over to host the European Grand Prix as the final round of the World Championship. This was a fall-back event, staged only when the Portuguese Grand Prix organizers at Estoril were unable to complete circuit improvements in time to retain their fixture.

By common consensus, Jerez is hardly the place of which legends are made. With the F1 circus used to celebrating its seasonal finales at such spectacular circuits as Suzuka or Adelaide, it will be hard pressed to avoid being labelled as an anti-climax.

The grid lines prior to the start of the 1990 Spanish Grand Prix at Jerez.

First published in Great Britain, 1997
by George Weidenfeld & Nicolson Ltd
The Orion Publishing Group
5 Upper St Martin's Lane
London WC2H 9EA

A CIP catalogue record for this book is available from the British Library.

ISBN: 0 297 82264 0

Designed by The Design Revolution

Edited by Jonathan Hilton